T0326600

Dragon's Lair and the
Fantasy of Interactivity

Dragon's Lair and the Fantasy of Interactivity

MJ Clarke

LEXINGTON BOOKS

Lanham • Boulder • New York • London

Published by Lexington Books
An imprint of The Rowman & Littlefield Publishing Group, Inc.
4501 Forbes Boulevard, Suite 200, Lanham, Maryland 20706
www.rowman.com

86-90 Paul Street, London EC2A 4NE, United Kingdom

British Library Cataloguing in Publication Information Available

Library of Congress Cataloging-in-Publication Data

Names: Clarke, M. J. (Michael Jordan), 1979- author.
Title: Dragon's Lair and the fantasy of interactivity / MJ Clarke.
Description: Lanham, Maryland : Lexington Books, [2022] | Includes bibliographical references and index. | Summary: "This book revives a neglected video game classic through a critical examination of its design, its makers, its recording medium, and its imagery. The investigation of these facets reveals a game shaped by the demands of its context and is instructive for contemporary debates in media studies"—Provided by publisher.
Identifiers: LCCN 2022011925 (print) | LCCN 2022011926 (ebook) | ISBN 9781793636034 (Cloth) | ISBN 9781793636041 (ePub) Subjects: LCSH: Dragon's Lair (Game) | Video games—Design.
Classification: LCC GV1469.35.D73 C53 2022 (print) | LCC GV1469.35.D73 (ebook) | DDC 794.8/3—dc23/eng/20220405
LC record available at https://lccn.loc.gov/2022011925
LC ebook record available at https://lccn.loc.gov/2022011926

For my parents,
Thanks for all the quarters

Contents

Acknowledgments

This book was made possible with the generous support of the College of Arts and Letters at California State University, Los Angeles, which awarded me both a Research, Scholarship, and Creative Activity Award in fall 2017 and a Faculty Sabbatical in fall 2021.

Initially conceived as a "quick book" that could be designed and executed relatively quickly, this book was complicated by the predictable predictabilities of life and the snowballing complications of research. I am humbly grateful to all the people in my life who helped this book, in big ways and small, finally come into being. Special thanks should be reserved for my students at Cal State LA who have provided me refreshing inspiration over the years, particularly those graduate students who attended my graduate seminar in "Media During the 1980s" and the many others who have tolerated my courses in "New Media" which provided me with the space and opportunity to present and reflect upon many of the ideas found within these pages. Thanks to my brother-in-law James, the consummate gamer, who found for me a physical copy of *Dragon's Lair* to play on my PS4. Thanks to Jeff Kinder and Dave Hallock, creators of the online *Dragon's Lair* Project, who have maintained a quick resource that was invaluable to me as I was unpacking the design of the game. Jeff Goad Ngo Vinh-Hoi, producers of the podcast *The Appendix N Book Club*, provided a lot of inspiration for the book's look into fantasy literature found in chapter 4. Also, many thanks go to my editor Jessica Tepper and readers at Lexington Books who have been patiently supportive of the project through its extended timeline.

But, most importantly, the existence of this book—comparatively modest it is in scope and ambition—is a testament to the profound love of Ester, Fritzi, and Robin that I have been unduly fortunate enough to experience.

Introduction

The opening minutes of season two of *Stranger Things* wonderfully depicts both the agony and the ecstasy of classic arcade gaming. A frantic montage follows the series' four protagonists as they scramble for loose change and optimistically rush to the local arcade. The four friends meet and huddle around a single game cabinet, but within seconds of gameplay it is over, sending the user, Dustin, into a fit of profanity: "overpriced bullshit—piece of shit!" Notably, the game that they are playing (and cursing) is Don Bluth and Rick Dyer's *Dragon's Lair* (1983).

The game was an obvious choice; perhaps no arcade game is so nostalgically remembered yet so critically bemoaned. A bit of a technological neanderthal, *Dragon's Lair* implemented a unique combination of videogame components and home video replay, garnering great popular media and user attention at a moment of contracted economic returns and popularity for the videogame arcade business. But subsequently, writers and critics have cast the game as a cautionary tale of bad game design which left users spending most of their time watching rather than doing, which utilized a system that only occasionally scanned for user input, and which activated a game narrative that deployed repeated rooms and obstacles, all complicating emerging ideas around interactivity in both media studies and practice.

The strange case of *Dragon's Lair* offers a provocative conundrum to the emerging discipline of videogame history. In Erkki Huhtamo's (2005) genealogy of arcade machines of the late nineteenth and early twentieth centuries, the historian sketched the division of these devices into two broad functions: the automatic, a tradition of marveling at the "untouchable" as in the case of automatons and elaborate store window displays, and the proto-interactive, which gave users the "largely illusory, feeling of being in command" in mutoscopes, slot machines, and other mechanical games (8). While Huhtamo acknowledges that early amusement parks freely intermingled these two machine experiences, the construction and execution of *Dragon's Lair* demonstrates that their segregation into dedicated objects was never so simple and required negotiation. In this simple manner, *Dragon's Lair* already offers a productive wrinkle to smooth, standardized, linear timelines of technical progress and efficiency, offering an ideal site to conduct what Siegfried Zielinski termed "media variantology." In this loose methodology, Zielinski zooms in on lost experiments and presumed failures of the deep media past not to preserve them as curious but to lay bare the often-neglected heterogeneity of media change and to "discover fractures or turning points in historical master plans that provide useful ideas for navigating the labyrinth of what is currently firmly established" (7). Similarly, Raiford Gains (2014), in his exhaustive archival examination of another early game experiment later dubbed *Tennis for Two*, advocates against the utility of "linear narratives of video game history," highlighting instead a method that outlines media change as "a complex of disparate, isolated events not easily plotted in a progressing timeline" (102).

In this book, I plan likewise to recuperate *Dragon's Lair* as a fascinating textual experiment or variant interlaced with powerful industrial strategies, institutional discourse, and textual desires around key notions of interactivity and fantasy. Creating a multifaceted, historical study of the game considering its design, makers, recording medium, and manifest content, I will suggest that the more appropriate metaphor for *Dragon's Lair* is not that of a neanderthal but a socio-technical network, infusing and advancing debates about the production and consumption of new screen technologies in the manner of a scientific experiment. More specifically, I contend that *Dragon's Lair* acts as an early "threshold format" (Hughes 2016) that, through its implementation and construction, interrogated the emerging transition from old to new media as an industrial question, a creative conundrum, a spectatorial reconsideration, and a political-economic urgency. My book then responds to a growing academic interest in early gaming history (Wolf 2012; Guins and Lowood 2016; Newman 2017) as well as media archeology (Parikka 2012; Huhtammo 1997) in casting *Dragon's Lair* as an open moment of historical indecision. In the first case, the game provoked and was provoked by structural changes in the media industries that prompted reconsiderations into who would work within and on the format of videogames as well as what physical media should be deployed in their construction. In the second case, this uncertainty complicated the core questions at the heart of *Dragon's Lair*'s construction around game design, narrative, and look. And lastly, *Dragon's Lair* offered a way for its makers and users to reconsider their relationship to screen media, becoming one of several contemporary media innovations that attempted to frame so-called interactivity and imagine a new user subjectivity more copacetic with the emerging neoliberal worldview in a cultural sphere still dominated by mass-mediated experiences. In other words, far from being the gaming failure posited by evolutionary-minded lay critics, *Dragon's Lair* offers a fascinating provisional solution to still unsettled questions of media technology. The game, its history, and its legacy then all exist as an overdetermined site of imaging or, like Foucault's panopticon, as a ghost technology that, in the critical eyes of the historian, is more about the needs and crises of institutional change, discursive order, and subject creation than anything like supposed artistic value or long-term financial success.

In chapter 1, I first examine how the arcade machine's hybrid platform, a specifically engineered system that incorporated both traditional media and computing elements, shaped the finished game's design choices. Drawing on a close analysis of the game's technical and schematic documents as well as sample gameplay, this chapter suggests how *Dragon's Lair*, like all videogames, manages signal timing and multiple temporalities, and how this game specifically incorporates timing itself directly in gameplay. Focusing specifically on the essential incorporation of the videodisc drive, which guaranteed *Dragon's Lair* its distinct look and competitive advantage, the chapter concludes with a consideration of how this component both prevented the game from employing already established game design elements, yet also encouraged the innovation of several novel techniques of design. First, the videodisc's capability for frame address allowed for non-linearity in event sequencing, a technique undergirded by several visual and narrative choices committed by *Dragon's Lair*'s makers. And, second, the videodisc's rich, hand-drawn imagery allowed for the creation of dense optical puzzles as game obstacles, ostensibly equating watching with activity, a theoretical equation in step with then-contemporary advances in academic media theory.

In chapter 2, I conduct a deep contextual production history of the making of the game. Through an investigation of industrial trade information, I suggest that the unique and disorganized division of labor that constructed the game, and overdetermined its design, can be unpacked with an understanding of deeper structural changes of its historical moment. Specifically, the chapter demonstrates how crisis and uncertainty, along with an overall sense of entrepreneurial possibility, in tacitly connected media industries including the videogame, the animation, the feature film, and the animation businesses, informed the game's conception and execution. The chapter concludes with a consideration of the immediate success and rapid demise of *Dragon's Lair* as its makers were drawn into the next fad and fashion in the boom-and-bust media electronics field, namely the rush toward the home computer.

In chapter 3, I situate the legacy of the game in a larger discursive analysis around the then-emerging concept of interactivity itself which congealed around the new medium of videodiscs. *Dragon's Lair* was just one of many experiments that attempted to use this new recording medium to reimagine the production and consumption of media as a so-called interactive experience. In this chapter, I first compare *Dragon's Lair* to several contemporary patents concerning the application of videodiscs in order to distill the specific historical significance of interactivity for these inventors. Next, the chapter looks at two other famous "failed" entrepreneurial attempts to use videodiscs to move from so-called old media to new—Robert Abel's *CubeQuest* and Lucasfilm's *Editdroid*—to better understand the industrial zeal for interactive media across screen industries. And, lastly, I use historical documents to suggest a political-economic critique of interactivity itself as not unique to gaming, but as a new normative subject position recurrent across powerful neoliberal institutions.

And, in chapter 4, I examine more closely the manifest visual and narrative surface to consider what cultural resources were deployed to elicit interactivity in potential users of the game. The game was part and parcel of a revival of a particular subgenre of fantasy, often called sword-and-sorcery, which used selected elements from a 1930s literary tradition in a manner which was both formally usefully and politically economically expedient, speaking again to the creation of new interactive subject position. Specifically, I connect *Dragon's Lair* to several hallmarks of this subgenre. Drawing on the writings of Fritz Leiber, I demonstrate how the game adapts sword-and-sorcery's adventuring protagonist. Through an examination of the work of Robert E. Howard, I explain how *Dragon's Lair* adapts the notion of spatial incursion, important to that author's sword-and-sorcery Conan stories. And lastly, I use the writings of Clark Ashton Smith to show how the game re-used sword-and-sorcery's uniquely grim worldview, offering stories of not "happily ever after," but of nihilistic failure.

As indicated, the book will employ a holistic methodology that integrates and interweaves inquiry of design, industry, medium, and imagery. And while the manuscript speaks broadly to media change in the 1980s, it also will offer a critical model of how to examine comprehensively a single gaming text. Although game studies has expanded by leaps and bounds in the last 20 years, there are relatively few books devoted to single titles. Recently, MIT Press has commenced a series devoted to so-called platform studies that examine specific gaming and computing hardware systems (such as Bogost and Montfort (2009) on the Atari VCS and Aresenault (2017) on the Super Nintendo), and a small number of books from the University of Michigan's Landmarks of Video Games Series have devoted minute critical focus to a number of important gaming titles (like Perron (2012) on the *Silent Hill* series and Pincheck (2013) on *Doom* (1993)), but still monographs centered on single gaming titles are quite rare. My hope is that this project will provide a model as well as inspiration to future works focused on singular games comparable to the attention and care given to other media works.

Chapter 1

Dragon's Lair
The Platform

Dragon's Lair belongs to a small but significant set of videogames that, responding to larger financial uncertainty in the gaming industry, incorporated the emerging technologies of optical media and videodisc players,[1] in the specific case of this game either a Pioneer LD-V1000 or a PR-7820 laserdisc machine, to store and reproduce the game's audio and visual elements in a stable, un-manipulable format. To be sure, videogame systems historically have relied on commercially available televisual equipment for their operation—famously Nolan Bushnell's first *Pong* sets were simply hacked Sears black-and-white televisions without a microprocessor or a single portion of code (Lowood 2009). But *Dragon's Lair* and the handful of other videodisc-based games of the late 1970s and early 1980s acted as particular hybrid systems in which their specific form of data storage and retrieval figured prominently in the games' construction and also in their eventual design as well as their distinct and novel look, which incorporated "full-pictorial animation" (Dyer 1984) at a time when competing publishers still often relied on using a largely abstracted iconography to represent players, objects, and game worlds. Like the case of subsequent interactive movie games, *Dragon's Lair*'s "reliance on pre-made content has a deep structural impact" on the game's look, design, and experience (Lessard 2009, 197). The videodisc acted as a technical game engine providing access to unit operations (Bogost 2006) of cel animation, non-linear order, and filmic shot construction, discussed here. And, although many of these games' specific technical formats and design solutions were often disavowed in subsequent generations of gaming, they still act as instructive symptoms of a pre-convergence mediascape in which innovators sought to imagine and attempted to leverage new technologies and build a space for interactive users within old media systems, trackable in everything from contemporary two-way cable television systems to experiments in non-linear film. These games, as textual experiments, presciently pointed forward to a business climate in which the boundaries between respective media made less sense and in which the collaboration across these barriers, in the case of *Dragon's Lair* between a fledgling developer (Rick Dyer's RDI), a minor games publisher (Cinematronics), and an independent animator (Don Bluth), became the mandate of more recent media organizations. *Dragon's Lair* added to this agenda also by giving users lessons about limited input in cybernetic systems by directing desire through a premodern fantasy affect, then recurrent throughout contemporary popular culture. Yet, before the game can incite such historical evaluation or elicit such critical abstractions, the game should work.

DRAGON'S LAIR AS HYBRID PLATFORM

Videogames, as material objects and modular networks, operate by organizing a discrete set of electronic signals and representing them to a user as an experience of interactive and uninterrupted play imbued with simulated liveness to the game itself. A majority of these operations occur below the attention of the user as electric pulses pass through micron-width transistor gates or wait patiently at a buffer for the next microsecond system refresh. Or, as Friedlich Kittler (2012) has suggested, humans act as part of these electronic grids only in the last instance. The videogame's own internal hardware microprocessor along with its accompanying software logic both translate and orchestrate these rapid and discontinuous flashes into an emergent feeling of responsive control and continuous audiovisual output.[2] As Kyle Stine and Axel Volmar (2021) point out, "all machines whether mechanical, electronic, or symbolic are time machines" that "consolidate temporality" (9, 14). By this, the authors refer to machines' internal demand to order operations into sequence, their need to reconcile human and non-human actors into logical succession, and their work to mediate devices and innovations from across historical time. By looking more pointedly at the schematics of *Dragon's Lair*, we can track exactly these sorts of complicated temporal practices.

In their important book *Racing the Beam* (2009), Ian Bogost and Nick Montfort argue for the critical centrality of videogame systems' ability to condense and create temporalities by demonstrating the hardware affordances, or in the authors' terminology platform, of the Atari VCS. Specifically, the authors describe at length how this home gaming console was constructed with and enabled by a MOS Technology 6502 CPU coupled with a proprietary television interface adapter along with very little internal RAM to build and re-build continuous game experiences during the imperceptible, blank moments between the horizontal and vertical resetting, or blanking periods, of the connected NTSC television's electron scanning gun—thereby reconciling the temporalities of a late twentieth-century technology (silicon microprocessors) with that of an early twentieth-century device (the television). And while VCS's technical platform was originally built only for playing *Pong*, even including the code for creating visual paddles and balls within the system, crafty developers were able to stretch and manipulate the platform to create other types of games and experiences. But always central to the construction of these other VCS games, or ROMs, were the limitations and the capabilities of the console, or platform and, specifically, its ability to create uninterrupted play through disconnected pulses, or to condense multiple technical temporalities into one phenomenologically felt game and action time. Echoing these technical observations, Christopher Hanson (2018), in his book on videogames and time, adapts the term liveness from television studies to discuss the temporal experience of games. In television studies liveness denotes that the feeling of immediacy and intimacy in TV broadcast is a textual and, arguably, ideological effect of programming and not simple inherent property of the medium (see, e.g., Feuer 1983). The work of Atari programmers, as described by Bogost and Montfort, suggest the same for the creation of liveness in gaming.

Like home game consoles, coin-operated arcade videogame machines, too, can be understood as gaming platforms with unique capabilities based on electronic components; however, unlike consoles creators, arcade developers build their machines for more limited uses, constructing games that act as purpose-built, rarified platforms onto themselves. This rarification can take the form of novel input controls such as *Centipede*'s (1980) track ball or *Digital Dance Revolution*'s (1998) dance pad or a unique visual output system as in *Battlezone*'s (1980) periscope viewfinder or *Time Traveler*'s (1991) holographic display. The same differentiation also applies to the internal architecture of arcade games. For example, Brett Camper (2012) has examined the so-called Williams arcade platform, a technological protocol that the same-named publisher used in several releases from the early 1980s (*Defender* (1981), *Joust* (1982), *Robotron 2084* (1982)). In this work, the author demonstrated how that platform's chip set, powered by a 1 mhz, 8-bit Motorola 6809E, and limited RAM capacity, combined with the informal mandate of uninterrupted play, resulted in several technical-aesthetic solutions and a consequent Williams look and feel. Simply put, this platform used batch, repeating tile sets to represent game objects and not the more memory-consuming system of objects and sprites, which would eventually become standardized in arcade games, creating a sparse playfield (all three cited games take place on fields of black) and a distinct sensation of speed and momentum in avatar movement. Additionally, the platform enabled the application of object color switching and particle explosion visual effects—both techniques unavailable to contemporary platforms using sprite graphics. In other words, while platforms are designed primarily to manage signal timing, the specific way in which this timing is achieved has a fateful effect upon the look, design and experience of the games run on it, as in both the case of Atari's VCS as well as the Williams arcade platform.

Dragon's Lair's own hybrid platform, while significantly different in its incorporation of optical media, also demonstrates architectural isomorphism with contemporary arcade games, specifically in its choice of CPU. The game's timing and operations are managed by a Zilog Z-80A 8-bit microprocessor. Designed by a small group of ex-Intel engineers and financed largely by Exxon Oil, the Z-80 series served as a near industry co-standard, along with the MOS Tech 6502, as a result of the chip set's robust design, its shared programming protocol with Intel's own 8080 microprocessor, and perhaps most importantly its modest price point of $200 upon its 1975 launch (Slater 2007). Subsequently the chip set appeared in a multitude of important games from *Mario Bros* (1983) to *Galaga* (1981) as well as several gaming consoles from the Sega Master System (1985) to the original Nintendo Game Boy (1989). *Dragon's Lair*'s Z-80, with its 16 lines of outgoing address and eight outgoing-incoming lines for data, is used to communicate with an 8-position joystick, a single action button, a 32K ROM cartridge, 2K variable RAM, a separate sound synthesis generator, and the laserdisc player itself. The CPU contains a 4-Mhz clock and a real-time clock which interrupts the platform's operations every 33 microsecond to ensure the system's synchronization both with the laserdisc player and its video output, which was sent to a 19-inch Wells-Gardner monitor—another typical arcade game component—running the standard NTSC display rate of 29.97 frames per second. Unlike some gaming platforms which must re-calculate at a monitor's horizontal reset between individual scan lines, *Dragon's Lair* only readdresses the system in the longer vertical pause at every frame advancement to re-check game ROM and laserdisc synchronization. And because nearly all of the game's visual and audio data is both stored and played directly from the laserdisc, the need for ROM storage and RAM capacity is relatively modest. For example, another fantasy-themed arcade game released only one year later, Capcom's *Ghosts and Goblins*, was overseen by a 8-bit Motorola 68809 CPU but also necessitated additional 40K RAM and six 16-bit ROM chips to store and reproduce the game's objects (avatars, enemies, projectiles, score, etc.) as well as another 16K of RAM and another six 16-bit ROM chips to store and reproduce the game's scrolling backgrounds (Capcom USA 1986). *Dragon's Lair*, obviously, needed no such components.

The demands and functions of the platform were considerably more simple and refined to the central business of condensing multiple electronic, mechanical, and human temporalities into an uninterrupted play experience incorporating textual liveness and user action. Again, the *Dragon's Lair* operation board interrupts itself and repopulates its RAM every vertical refresh or every 33 microseconds checking coin credits, player order, player score, game state, and whether the connections of the user's controls are making contact. And vitally the RAM operations also query checks the discrete frame location encoded on the game's dedicated laserdisc which contains most of the game's audio and visual information. The high-density laserdisc stores this information on lines which are 1.66 microns apart and read by a laser-guided head as the player revolves the platter at the rate of 750 RPMs or one revolution every 8 microseconds. The laserdisc contains visual information that, too, was meticulously timed by the work of hand-drawn animators who subdivided and decomposed character movement in distinct frames, typically 18 frames per second, to ensure the sensation of continuous action and time. The game presents users with this visual information along with constrained opportunities to respond with input which are either 1 second or 2 seconds long, either 30 or 60 processing cycles, or either 25- or 50-disc revolutions. The function of the platform is first and foremost to combine and reconcile these multiple temporalities into a single game experience.

DRAGON'S LAIR AND TIMING

However, *Dragon's* Lair's platform is unlike most other contemporary games because of its novel incorporation of stored media and because of its relationship to timing itself. Most platforms are designed to manage the timing of technical infrastructure of the game to allow for emergent gameplay, which can be either fast or slow paced, or more commonly combine some form of rhythmic alternation. In *Dragon's Lair* timing is the game itself.

Along with the release of *Dragon's Lair*, the platform and game's inventor Rick Dyer submitted a patent application to the World Intellectual Property Organization calling the game a "full pictorial animation videogame" and seeking legal protection from potential imitators from Western Europe, Australia, and Japan. Including a rough schematic of the cabinet's internal components and flow charts of its operational logic, the bulk of the report comprises an extended description of precisely how the game works. The document's author describes a Russian doll structure of nested temporalities—from represented narrative time, down to frame screen time, and down to clock time of the microprocessor—and how each is reconciled in the operation of the game through its use of what Dyer calls rooms, nodes, and windows. In the terminology of the report, a user enters represented rooms where they encounter visual representations of selection nodes in which a corrective action must be taken to overcome some visually represented obstacle or challenge, otherwise the user will "die" (or less colloquially, lose a try and reset the game). There are no second chances or hit points in *Dragon's Lair*—all of the game's nodes present pass-fail, Boolean scenarios. At these nodes, users are presented with timing windows, a limited portion of time in which they must engage the correct input action—either a joystick direction or a depression of the action button. To be exact, nodes are prompts of visual data operated by the laserdisc player, while windows are scans of physical input operated by the CPU. While many of these nodes demand a quick reflex and that a user respond as swiftly as possible to an accompanying visual cue, many other obstacles, such as the spinning cudgels (see fig. 1.1) or the rolling boulders that necessitate that a user act swiftly as well as within the exact appropriate window. But regardless of how the game cues prompt a user to respond, the available windows are short, either 1 or 2 seconds. The result is a game that combines waiting-acting in that order of prominence.[3]

To explain the interplay of rooms, nodes, and windows, the WIPO application describes, in both prose and in annotated illustrations, the room that users first encounter in 66% of gameplays of *Dragon's Lair*. In this room, the user finds their avatar, Dirk the Daring, perched on a narrow ledge overseeing an enormous pit of fire and traversable only by way of a set of pendulum vines (see figs. 1.2 and 1.3)—an obstacle probably already familiar to many gamers who experienced similar events in the arcade game *Jungle Hunt* (1982) and the console game *Pitfall* (1982). After a wide shot establishing the breadth of the pit and the room, the game cuts to a close-up of Dirk's feet on a stone ledge that slides into the wall, diminishing the

Figure 1.1   Swinging Cudgels in *Dragon's Lair* (2017). *Source*: Screenshot Captured from the Digital Leisure PS4 Port.

Figure 1.2   Swinging Vine Room in _Dragon's Lair_ (2017). _Source_: Screenshot Captured from the Digital Leisure PS4 Port.

Figure 1.3   Swinging Vine Room Insert in _Dragon's Lair_ (2017). _Source_: Screenshot Captured from the Digital Leisure PS4 Port.

avatar's already precarious footing and giving a visual representation of the game's clock—something must happen before the ledge entirely disappears. Next, a successful user is able to move from this ledge to the swinging ropes moving from one to the next as they approach one another in set of individual shots; in this case something must happen in "precisely the right time" (Dyer 1983, 7). In this first room, the game exposes users to the two core strategies of gameplay: move fast but move at a precise time. And these nodes (jumping from rope to rope) are prompted with representational visual cues (the shrinking ledge, the approaching next rope) in advance of the non-representational infrastructural window. As the game progresses nodes become more or less generous in their prompting and in at least a handful of examples are willfully misleading, for example, the potion reading "drink me" should not be drunk (see fig. 1.4). Collectively, the vacillating prompts of the game's nodes, combined with the active window of 1 or 2 seconds of real time, constitute the experiential time of gameplay including discernible visual events and reaction of human players through input devices. To a user this time is experienced as rapid, but it is, of course, the most sluggish of the platform's interlocking temporalities.

The actual timing of the game's windows is much more constrained. As mentioned earlier, the windows are clocked at 1 or 2 seconds and the game is able to open and close them by checking the individual frame being read from the laserdisc and the statuses of the input device's connections every 33 microseconds, that is, every system interrupt or every screen refresh. In other words, each node contains either 30 or 60 individual frames or microprocessor cycles. In form and function, the windows mimic the if-not Boolean logic of the game's internal transistor gates discriminating single correct responses with everything else (waiting too long, moving too late, and moving incorrectly). For the game to work, or plainly for nodes to match windows, the computer and media components must remain in complete synchronization. And this is made possible by the laserdisc's ability to store individual frame

Figure 1.4   "Drink Me" in *Dragon's Lair* (2017). *Source*: Screenshot Captured from the Digital Leisure PS4 Port.

address and additional information on each of the platter's individual 54,000 still frames along with a ROM chip that stores window and solution information on each pertinent frame as well as a modest RAM site to store current frame and window information as games are played. Thus, underneath narrative time or a sequence of represented spaces, events, and obstacles, there is a frame time electro-mechanically facilitated (as in the case of the precursor technologies of film and television) and electronically tracked and stored. Or, the electronic metadata that would become standard for all digital media files becomes the technique to build a game.

TIMING AND TURBULENCE

In his McLuhan-influenced examination of media change and perception, Friedlich Kittler ([1986] 2006) discusses the interlocking invention of nineteenth-century technologies—grammophones, film, and typewriters—which fragmented the synthetic whole and monopoly of the lone previous media technology, the word, into a Lacanian triumvirate of the real, imaginary, and symbolic, respectively. In each case, the function was largely determined by the discourse around each new technology but also by the very sampling rate or timing, of each, from recorded audio's continuous analogue signal to the discrete and discontinuous "flow" of the film strip. Writing at roughly the same time as *Dragon's Lair*'s initial release, Kittler already forecast a coming media convergence where these differences of discourse, sampling, and function would re-coalesce around a shared, pre-symbolic binary code transmitted on vast systems of fiber optic networks. Through the schematics and the discussion of the work of timing in both *Dragon's Lair*'s internal architecture and design, we can trace an early and instructive attempt to achieve this technical convergence prior to ubiquitous digitalization.

Dragon's Lair, like most electronic games, necessitates sophisticated computational timing, however, as suggested, timing constitutes the game itself. Gameplay is managed by collapsing the narrative time of nodes, represented in visual "clocks" (shrinking platforms, swinging ropes) and embodied in user response; frame time as the platform tracks and stores laserdisc frame information; and computational time that translates narrative track time into a series of discrete and buffered instructions written and re-written into temporary system storage.[4] And it is the fusion of these multiple temporalities which generates a sense of uninterrupted play, central in Huizinga's (1933) ideal-typical conception of the phenomenon which poses the experience of play as one of consistent separation from the rule boundaries of everyday life. In his important examination of the apparatus of film, Giles Deleuze (1986) discusses that medium's ability to achieve an indirect image of time through combing immobile sections of any-time-whatsoever through different historical techniques of montage. The gap or interval between images, the gulf between wanting and doing, become the realm of the affect and a representation of unapproachable change, but also for Deleuze, of consciousness itself. Extrapolating to cybernetic systems like *Dragon's Lair*, the interval asymptotically pervades in the gaps of visual nodes, between filmic windows and computational pulses, a significant observation in a mediasphere dominated by seemingly real-time devices such as videogames and smartphones as well as protocols such as streaming, flattering users with a sense of constant control and instantaneous connectedness. Technological phenomenologists since Martin Heidegger have suggested that tools are those things that only come into consciousness when they break down; perhaps then this game can serve as an instructive example of how its work of collapsing temporalities, a presumption in the era of ubiquitous digitalization is made difficult by its hybrid construction and allows the interval to re-emerge as the site of all mediated experience.

A close reading of *Dragon's Lair*'s operational logic demonstrates that this game, like all complex information systems, is replete with non-human actors. Even in an example as relatively simple and elegant as this one, human input occurs only in the last instance and subsequent to a multitude of calculations. The multiple temporalities of *Dragon's Lair*'s logic also suggest that the consequence of digitalization is not simply a speeding up of social, economic, and cultural systems with human processors struggling to keep up, but also, echoing postmodern theory, the exposure of time itself is a complex socially constructed term emblemizing a multitude of experiences. Critical theorists Stine and Volmar (2021) call this both the palimpsest of temporal regimes and the uneven geography of social temporalities. Indeed, if the modernist project was to use empirical science and the technology of the machine to institute a standardized, rationalized, and progressive time, then the postmodern project used the metaphor of digital communication as well as media and information networks to think about the differential aspects of time, experienced as flows, distributed unevenly, and synchronized only with tremendous effort and occasional backlash.[5] For example, another prominent McLuhanite, sociologist Manuel Castells has described our contemporary experience of so-called real virtuality as one dominated by a fluid space of flows and timeless time in which both these fundamental modernist notions have been liquefied, thanks largely to digital networks. However, Castells doesn't cast these new notions as unifying but instead leaves room for what the theorist calls "spaces of place" and dark spots on the network grid (the fourth world in geopolitical terms) that demonstrate the dispersion of these core lifeworld experiences. Symptomatically, *Dragon's Lair* works similarly creating a sense of uninterrupted play not only through the technical collapsing of multiple temporalities but also by relying on the premodern iconography of fantasy and fairy tales which combined its own brand of timelessness through repeated units and figures (Claude Levi-Stauss's (1955) mythemes); its exposition and rhetoric ("once upon a time"); and through its mnemonically repeated sequences (Vladimir Propp's ([1958] 2012) codes) with placeful-ness through their connection to localized legend and folklore.

Avoiding larger philosophical discussions, we can at least suggest that contemporary notions of continuous time situate it less as an independent variable and more as another shared social notion that must be discursively supported, consistently re-articulated, and technologically standardized by way of both human and non-human agencies. Bruno Latour and the collective theorists of Actor Network Theory have developed a methodology that contends that most social analysis too quickly relies upon reified social abstractions without attending to the human and technological exchanges that undergird these larger notions, constituting a re-examination of the micropolitics in the work of social explanation. Game systems like *Dragon's Lair* provide ideal social-technical examples of Latour's ANT at work, achieved by thousands of non-human agents interlaced and fused with cultural intentions and traditions from notions of competition and violence as well as conventions of storytelling and visual composition.[6] The result is a complex melange that miraculously makes sense with emergent properties such as gameplay, game narrative, and uninterrupted play. But this last emergent property is only achieved through synchronization, coordination, and standardization, not dissimilar to Latour's own discussion of the work of scientific labor's own standardization that demands human coordination and technical prostheses (2005, 2013). In his canonical essay "Technology Is Society Made Durable" (1990), Latour uses the mundane example of hotel keys (a better example for American readers might be the bathroom key found at gas stations) where the social program (or intention) is to stop key disappearance and the technological agency is the annoying weight attached to the key to prevent any such theft. However, even in this simple example, there is an anti-program, the will not to return based on lassitude, indifference, defiance, or whatever. If the program of the network of *Dragon's Lair* is designed to create uninterrupted play, then can we similarly detect any anti-programs at work, or are there any dark spots on the grid?

As mentioned earlier, *Dragon's Lair* was built using an over-the-counter laserdisc player, which gave the game its novel look and competitive advantage but also created several problems for the maintenance of the uninterrupted play. At the time of the game's release, quick adoption of new media devices like these laserdiscs, and more importantly the VHS player, were familiarizing consumers with non-linear temporal control of data flow with pause, fast forward, and rewind functions. However, in *Dragon's Lair* these functions were locked away from the user and instead became adapted as a core mechanic of the gameplay. The imperfect cooperation of electronic, mechanical, and human inputs in the game's system occurs in the game's idiosyncratic problem of so-called blanking between rooms and between shots. Structurally, the game is organized around a set of rooms, or narrative spaces, each with one or more nodes. All these rooms (with the exception of the final one) both begin and end with the image or a door or other portal in order to better fuse the rooms together with a sense of continuous space and time. Moreover, each room is depicted with one or more conventional film shots, in which multiple shots are stitched together with classical filmmaking grammar of changes in shot scale, angle, and the virtual "camera's" spatial relationship to the subject matter, which also project a sense of continuous space and time. However, these attempts to maintain textual continuity are complicated by the physical distance of the differing frame locations on the spinning laserdisc as the laser head struggles to find the beginning of the next room or the proper solution but inevitably displays a momentary blank screen, often accompanied by a slight vertical roll, as it transitions to the next room or moment. The physical geography of the *Dragon's Lair* laserdisc was designed to minimize this problem within rooms by writing a perfect playthrough of nodes and their correct solutions adjacently on the disc itself; therefore, a perfect run-through of a room should prevent any screen blanking. And it is only the wrong moves which prompt a death animation stored at the end of the disc that force the data flow momentarily to pause as the playhead physically moves to the proper frame address. Therefore, a blanking event hypothetically would only occur in rooms when a death is imminent but often also occurs in the gaps between rooms. This was a unique error of micromoments of non-use in periods of use of media consumption (fundamentally different than turns where players wait but are still playing), but would become more common in an era of vaster network systems incorporating media—a problem of turbulence (Bryant 2007) colloquially known as buffering.

Turbulence in the system is present not only in the transitions between rooms and the shift from playing and "dying." Even if the correct keystrokes are made at the appropriate nodes within the computational windows, the visual output of the game often produces what writers in the film studies tradition consider continuity errors or jump cuts. Objects in the picture frame are spatially transposed between shots of conventionalized difference to an extent not accounted for in the visual record. Many analysts of film have remarked upon the historical importance of minimizing these perceived errors to maintain a sense of continuous narrative time and space, essential to the aesthetic logic and ideological project of classical film storytelling (Bordwell et al. 1985; Wollen 1986); yet, it is arguably less important in today's dominant styles of organizing visual narrative information (Shaviro 2010). Regardless of whether such so-called errors have become now commonplace, such was less likely the case upon *Dragon's Lair*'s 1983 release. These errors were unique to this game and the small group of other videodisc games. Conversely, sprite-based games, which store objects and animation loops in ROM memory and write them in RAM, visually "move" their objects across the raster screen surface through calculations and accompanying transpositions that consequentially create a sense of continuous movement and gives a user (like a film spectator) a movement image or an indirect image of continuous time.[7]

Dragon's Lair's first room (in 66% of games)—the previously described rope swinging sequence—immediately reveals these visual gaps. In this room, the user must move from one rope to the next, and the successful response to each node-window advances the shot to the next node. However, at each of the successive nodes the game recycles the same full shot of Dirk swinging three times. Moving between the gap from one rope to the next results in a cut from one shot to the next, each with precisely the same shot scale and angle—the traditional recipe for the jump cut. Inevitably, a visual gap is detectable as users have a window of 24 or 48 frames to activate the prescribed move, while proper match cuts, in cases with no shot difference, must be near frame perfect. This visual tic recurs in other rooms throughout the game. For example, another room depicts Dirk paddling his canoe around a series of whirlpools in an underground river where a player must respond by pressing left and right alternatively to avoid them. Yet even if the correct keystroke is made within the window, a shot change, depicting the same frame and scale, moves Dirk's paddle instantaneously from his left side to the right or vice versa—a clear example of what from the perspective of film studies is a continuity error. And even in cases where the shot scale and frame shift at selection nodes to allow for traditional match cutting, conventionalized film continuity is infrequently achieved. In this case, the penultimate cut of the crypt room is instructive. Here Dirk draws his sword to repel a group of ghosts, but a cut moves the avatar from the outer compositional and diegetic edge to the middle of the room. Similarly, in the collapsing bridge room, a user only sees the beginning and the conclusion of a jump across a collapsing chasm, subtracting the implied movement itself between shots.[8] I do not list all these examples to suggest that *Dragon's Lair* should be marked as a failure but simply to demonstrate that conventionally continuous movement, a traditional indicator of continuous space-time in film, TV, and videogames is complicated as a symptom of *Dragon's Lair*'s complex, pre-convergence system.

Moreover, I am not suggesting that *Dragon's Lair* as a platform was misguided or faulty but that, like Bogost, Montfort, and Camper, the platform contained a set of unique technical limitations that informed a set of novel solutions which shaped the game's design. The use of hand-drawn cell animation stored on a laserdisc, the achievement of so-called full-pictorial animation constituted the competitive advantage and novelty of the game in a moment of diminishing returns for the industry in which exploiting new organizational arrangements and emerging technologies of interactivity presented possible solutions. However, the latter also presented obvious complications for the game's makers. In the first case, hand-drawn animation is a very labor-intensive and, thus, an expensive process (especially before the complete decampment of American animation work to East Asia described in chapter 2). Contemporary reports cite the cost of the game's animation alone at around $1.2 million (Crook 1984); this is all the more significant coming at a time when the tasks of art and animation were still mostly the additional responsibility of programmers and developers and not yet a distinct subspecialty or budget item in videogame work. Technical limitations of the laserdisc platter, as already indicated, also complicated the game's design. The disc for *Dragon's Lair* was only able to hold approximately 37 1/2 minutes of game footage. And since the cabinet's screen was hardwired to the laserdisc player, the game had no ability to superimpose imagery on-the-fly. And lastly, because the visual output of the game was a filmed record, the game could not give the user the sensation of continuous control[9] typical of contemporary videogames and still cited as a critical marker of quality videogame design.[10]

Faced with these parameters, the makers of *Dragon's Lair* crafted a series of workarounds and adaptations. For example, a pre-rendered visual output made it impossible for the game to update a player's score onscreen; therefore, Dyer and his collaborators installed a separate LED score counter into the game cabinets. Meanwhile the look of the game field, un-littered by score tallies, verbal cues, or level indicators, became another marker of difference for the game and a subsequently influential aesthetic choice for later games evidenced in the lack of so-called heads up displays, map screens, or inventory subscreens in the games of Delphine Software (*Another World* (1991) and *Flashback* (1992)) as well as Sony's work with developer Fumito Ueda (*Ico* (2001), *Shadow of the Colossus* (2005), *The Last Guardian* (2016)). Also, since the cost of hand-drawn animation was so high, the game makers found a crafty way of re-using many rooms simply by inverting the visual image along the horizontal axis, making a left movement solution into a right movement and vice versa. Here the game mimes the innovations of limited animation in film and TV production wherein cost-conscious producers sped up and reduced cost of product by, for one, re-using previous work with repeated actions and backgrounds, an ironic choice given Bluth's public missives against this work style as discussed in the next chapter.

However, I contend that the two most important innovations or workarounds of *Dragon's Lair* can be found in the game's particular use of non-linearity and filmic puzzles.

DRAGON'S LAIR AND NON-LINEARITY

For both economic and technical reasons, in many early arcade games there exists an unalterable order of events both within levels, which is often overseen by onscreen and offscreen timers, and between levels, in which level two follows level one and level three follows level two and so on. Moreover, many elements in early arcade games are built around a core logic of linear timers—you can time the exit of ghosts from the center panel of *Pac-Man* (1980)—and calculations based on previous states—objects in these games do not "move" as much as the system transposes them and supplements this transposition with animation loops—and these calculations depend on a clear, consistent before and after. As explained earlier, a single play of *Dragon's Lair*, unique among its contemporaries, is built around a series of rooms which contain one or more selection nodes but which in themselves have no set order. The makers of the game took advantage of the non-linear access of the videodisc drive in which the point of address could be quickly shifted without complicating game calculations. According to the creator of the "*Dragon's Lair* Project," a fan-constructed website, the sequence of rooms in *Dragon's Lair* does follow a set playthrough, but each successive room is chosen from a variable list of two or three choices, giving the sensation of randomness (Kinder and Hallock, nd). Specifically, choices of 2 or 3 possible rooms in a game session sequence of 13 rooms, which must be completed to access the final boss room, gives users access to over one million unique room combinations—but this just describes the perfect playthrough. Game randomness is compounded by user death which could be programmed to reset the sequence of rooms at a different start point. In its preset specifications, *Dragon's Lair* restarts a user who has just died within the same room that they previously failed. Dyer's WIPO document even describes a game operation in which a user, subsequent to their death would be shown an alternative flash forward visually relaying the correct movement to overcome the room's current nodes, but for either technical or economic reasons (to increase coin drop) the protocol was never implemented in the finished game. The repetition of the preset gameplay could also be altered by a dip switch setting. Dip switches are physical selectors located on arcade games PCBs (printed circuit boards) that are read every system refresh and are used to override a game's core logic, in most cases to modulate a game's difficulty. Contemporary games often contained dip switch settings that determined, for example, the point total or score necessary to be awarded additional lives or tries. *Dragon's Lair*, however, contains several unique dip switch settings, many with an eye toward maximizing profit in a post-crash moment such as progressive coin drop to continue to play in the manner of an old-fashioned pay phone telephone call as well as a 50-cent initial gameplay cost. And another setting sends restarting players to any room in the game (save the final boss room)—a relatively easy operation given the non-linear access in the game's internal laserdisc. While a handful of contemporary videogames, beginning with *Tempest* (1981), gave users the ability to choose their beginning level, usually a marker of difficulty (and, subsequently, the regular linear order of the game would commence from that point on), no other game of *Dragon's Lair*'s time transports a user to an entirely different level or a completely different represented area within the game narrative after a user death. Later, this type of spatially diffuse spawning would become standard in current MOBA (multiplayer online battle arena) games. In most early arcade games, advancement in level is incentivized with some combination of the interlocking promises of unlocking new objects, new object behaviors, new game fields, and even new modes of play or play mechanics. But in *Dragon's Lair* the new visual experience of subsequent rooms becomes the most powerful incentivization for advancement, likely encouraging the randomizing dip switch which gives a user access to this core pleasure while mitigating the often unforgiving difficulty of the game. Like all videogames, this one is also based on a set of finite visual parameters, but by using the non-linearity of the laserdisc to randomize room order in regular play and between tries in the proper dip switch setting, the game presents users with an experience of a procedurally generated game space, albeit built with a relatively modest number of variables. In other words, random access informs both the game's design as well as a user's desire to play it.

Given the frame address of the system's laserdisc, *Dragon's Lair*'s quasi-procedural generation was easily achieved as a technical protocol; yet, how could the game use pre-rendered visual output to stitch all these elements together on-the-fly to create a textually cohesive game world? The makers of *Dragon's Lair* deployed two elegant compositional and aesthetic solutions embedded within the art itself. In his famous textual analysis of *The Most Dangerous Game*, Thierry Kuntzel (1980) examined this film as a dense meaning-making system that fundamentally relied on the image and idea of the door (in fact the first shot of the film is one of a door) to regulate not only the movement of onscreen characters but also the characters' and spectators' access to narrative information itself. Kuntzel argues that the diegetic image of doors acts as semiotic grammar marks that hold the entire narrative system together; a similar argument could be made of the room transitions of *Dragon's Lair*. Of the 28 unique rooms of the game (discounting those created through optical inversion) only one ends with Dirk not passing through a door or some other portal (the geyser room concludes with the character exiting frame left). These images likewise act as connective tissue that fuses the inconsistent and illogical narrative space of the evil dragon's castle. In Jesper Juul's (2004) influential examination of videogames and time, the theorist describes the fissures of arcade gameplay as "unexpected jumps in world and time by way of unconnected levels and rounds" (132). But *Dragon's Lair*, with its use of textual portals and represented connections, complicates this generalization.

The game's depicted character and setting also help give shape to a game-play's non-linear construction. Using imagery including knights, kidnapped princesses, evil dragons, trolls, and magic potions, *Dragon's Lair* invokes the specific genre of sword-and-sorcery, then undergoing a strong trend in popular culture (discussed later in chapter 4) and more broadly the mode of fantasy and fairy tale storytelling. Critical work on these premodern narrative traditions has often focused on the modularity of their core elements, their use of repetition in their narratives, and their status as somehow pre-symbolic in meaning—all features that can likewise be traced through the game's unique design. In his important study of Russian folktales, Vladimir Propp (2012) argued that fairy tales are constructed using a limited set of variable events, which the author dubs functions, to tell a seemingly diverse and strange set of stories, a logic not dissimilar to *Dragon's Lair*'s own mixing and matching of preset rooms to create relatively novel experiences. And according to Propp's contemporary, Mikhail Bahktin (2014) these functions are often loosely held by a specific chronotope, a style of textual depiction of time and space, where each is minimized in their specificity ("once upon a time" and "in a land far, far away" utterances) and is accumulatively supplemented in a series of "then," or "next," or "many years later"—again a fair enough description of the bridging nodes of the game and the resultant idiosyncratic sense of narrative time and space. More recent critics of fairy tales and fantasy such as Jack Zipes (2013) have stressed that this mode of storytelling has been historically developed to be told extemporaneously to an audience, effecting its resultant narrative features. Specifically, these tales were often constructed with built-in mnemonic devices for the recounter such as defined modularity of possible elements, per Propp, a lack of spatiotemporal guide posting, per Bahktin, and the use of simple sequences and repetitions. Fairy tales often deploy lists and series to build characters and sequences (*Three Little Pigs*, *Seven Dwarves*, etc.), and *Dragon's Lair* mimics this technique through its own repetition and reshuffling of rooms played again and again. Moreover, many of the core elements of these older stories were the work of pre-literate creators and only subsequently put into linguistic, fixed form through the work of later Enlightenment-era collectors (Hans Christian Andersen and Brothers

Grimm). Subsequently several theorists have highlighted exactly this lineage
to explain how fairy tales are able to articulate and manage unconscious
desires (Bettelheim 1975) and suggest pre-linguistic segments of meaning
creation (Levi-Strauss 1955). Many arcade games of the era (and like other
earlier popular culture forms of the twentieth century before them such as
nickeodeons and comic strips) access this tradition by asking users to operate on a pre-symbolic register, using reflexive reaction to navigate the game
infrastructurally based not on deep symbolic meaning, but on binary choices
of off and on, correct and incorrect; in fact, the only time that linguistic signs
appear on the *Dragon's Lair* game field during play they are either distracting
(the rapids sign in the underground river room) or clearly misleading (again,
the potion that reads "drink me" should not be drunk). This game then emu-
lates the modular, repetitious, pre-linguistic features of fairy tale storytelling,
but it is in the last feature and its collision with gaming's so-called interactivity that constitute the platform's second challenge and responding innovation.

DRAGON'S LAIR AND FILMIC PUZZLES

It is true that *Dragon's Lair* is a game that outwardly gives a user very
limited control, but gameplay is not synonymous with control. Because of
the use of pre-rendered animation and the core gameplaying logic of nodes
and windows, only the single keystrokes committed at the appropriate game
windows have an effect on the game—and even that effect is a minimal,
binary choice of success or failure. Simply put, the user is not flattered with
the same agential feeling of seemingly continuous control that marks so
much of digital experience and is arguably central to its ideological function as discussed in chapter 3. But control is not interactivity. All electronic
videogames have prescribed limits, and most games, both electronic and
analogue, have relatively stable rule sets that are constructed specifically
to limit available actions.[11] The visual richness of *Dragon's Lair*, thanks to
full-pictorial animation, likely complicates this balance as it suggests a deep,
lush world of possibilities but, in the end, priorities only single actions. Dyer
himself discussed this problem of interactivity in his WIPO document in
which he contrasted his own game with those he termed as visually limited
by their "multiplicity of choices . . . [and their] virtually unlimited number
of permutations and combinations of action and interaction by the symboli-
cally related objects included within the game representation" (1). Instead,
Dragon's Lair presents "incidents being portrayed [that] include physical and
other constraints which severely limit the options available to the protagonist.
Thus, unlike the situation in *Pac-Man* or other maze-chase games the hero
. . . does not have many options" (8). Ironically, then a visually rich world

is necessarily supplemented with an inverse paucity in terms of choice. In fact, game design itself might be defined similarly as the elegant attenuation of available actions, but the weighing of this bargain seemingly haunted the designer. Dyer's next game, *Thayer's Quest* (1984), combined pre-rendered hand-drawn animation with narrative pauses with an entire keyboard of possible choices and coordinated actions (see fig. 1.5).

Dragon's Lair achieves this narrowing of user choice by inverting the conventional relationship of avatar and environment. In most contemporary arcade games, users were given a wide latitude of movement across single screen spaces and eventually horizontally or vertically scrolling screens. And in many cases mastery of represented space is tantamount to mastery of the game itself—get to the top, make it through, move to avoid, cover all the spaces, pick up all the tokens, and so on.[12] But in Dyer's game the seemingly stable background and environment suddenly acts upon the user and their avatar from avalanching ceilings, to collapsing floors, to disappearing stairs, to shrinking platforms, and electrified surfaces. Indeed, the game's rooms and their obstacles are replete with inanimate objects that spring to life to provide environmental dangers: the Lizard King's treasure box suddenly steals Dirk's sword, a statue of a blacksmith comes alive to attack the user (see fig. 1.6),

Figure 1.5 Keyboard of a Coin-Operated Machine of RDI's *Thayer's Quest* (1984).
Source: Photo by Author.

a bubbling cauldron produces a deadly apparition, and so on. Gameplay then entails quickly scanning and decisively reacting to environments and their objects rather than acting upon them.

Dragon's Lair also inverts the standards of contemporary game design in another interesting way. Arcade games of that era incentivized improvisation in play by giving players a constructed yet open multitude of continuous options of activity, or in Dyer's terminology a "multiplicity of options" (1). This means that no two sessions of play, or colloquially every "life," would never be entirely the same; however, while the exact circumstances of a lost life may differ, compositionally and visually every user death is precisely the same—Mario is touched, collision is activated, and he spins; Pac-Man is touched, collision is activated, and it implodes, and so on. But in *Dragon's Lair* every life is outwardly the same (accepting the non-linear room selection); yet, the game gives a plethora of death animations each depicting a contextually appropriate demise. A YouTube post claiming to depict every death animation runs for 3 minutes and 17 seconds, a significant portion of time for a laserdisc whose total running time was only 37 1/2 minutes and a game, which if played successfully, only lasts approximately 11 minutes. At the very least, this suggests one of the core pleasures of the game might be watching Dirk die in any number of spectacular ways rather than improvising him out of danger (discussed at greater length in chapter 4). In fact, this visual pleasure and death drive more recently has been reincorporated into many FPS games in the form of a kill cam which

Figure 1.6 Blacksmith Attack in *Dragon's Lair* (2017). *Source*: Screenshot Captured from the Digital Leisure PS4 Port.

allows user to view their own demise replayed to them from a distanced, third-person perspective.

The specific style of interactivity elicited in *Dragon's Lair* is reactive as a player spends most of their time scanning the environment and its objects. Current game lay criticism usually points to the game as an early example of so-called quick time events (QTE), and at least one critic claims that the game was just "one big quick time event" (Langshaw 2014). QTEs are events in videogames where a user must activate prescribed input combinations within timed windows, oftentimes in a manner atypical of the surrounding gameplay. However, I argue that the analytic distinction of QTEs is much too imprecise as many classic and most modern videogames contain moments of so-called twitch mechanics which test a user's ability to hit certain button combinations rapidly, an action that is only ever conventionally linked to onscreen events. In this sense QTE is less an anomalous gameplay segment, but more a simplified and refined of precisely what many videogames ask of their users. Moreover, calling a segment a QTE actually does little to specify how visual cues signal proper action response and what type of relationship there is between the visual output and the requested user input. In some QTEs there the relationship between cues and actions are minimal and arbitrary. For example, the *God of War* (2005–present) series contains several QTEs as the avatar autonomously moves onscreen and is accompanied with a superimposed icon of a button the user must press to continue. The timing and choice of button are mostly arbitrary with occasional contextual connections as, for example, when a player must press a button repeatedly to denote extreme physical avatar effort onscreen. More interesting examples of this type have attempted to marry cues and actions through a deeper connection of visual output and desired input as in, for example, *Heavy Rain* (2010) where users must time button mashes with depicted avatar footfalls and a controller shake with the shake of a medical inhaler. Arguably, mechanical arcade games, such as pinball, too constitute an analogue version of QTEs where cues and action are not arbitrarily connected or fused with represented character movement, but instead quiz a user's tacit sense of practical physics and geometry. Another class of games uses both tone and rhythm as a technique to fuse cue and action. The very popular *Guitar Hero* (2005–2015) and *Rock Band* (2007–2017) series as well as the *Parappa the Rappa* (1996) games synchronize QTE controls to the beat and the tone of popular music with both visual cues as signs to indicate proper variety of button hits; rhythmic cues as the song's relative tempos indicate the proper timing of button hits; and tonal cues as buttons are implicitly mapped as relative notes, tones, or lyrics. These music games clearly use timed windows, but the combination of cue and action and of output and input is complex. I argue that *Dragon's Lair*, thanks to its hybrid, pre-convergent media-computer construction presents another unique coupling of cue and action by testing a user's visual intelligence and more precisely their tacit understanding of cinematic codes and conventions.

Dragon's Lair is a game where a user watches and acts, in that order of prominence. Drawing on work by videogame designer Richard Rouse, James Newman (2004) in his examination of videogames argued that seemingly non-interactive moments of videogames are constitutive of the experience and subtractive to in it, stating "playing a videogame . . . involves often protracted periods that prima facie, do not appear to bear the traits of 'play'" (76). In his analysis, Newman specifically points to the technical and functional importance of the conventional downtime of so-called level breaks which are used to reset internal systems and offer a respite to tally score or resolve narrative. Similarly, David O'Grady (2013) argues that "many dynamic systems—and certainly many video games—juxtapose moments of action and great potential for agency with more contemplative moments of observation, reflection, and evaluation" (110). In his useful book on videogame theory, Alexander Galloway (2006) provides a provocative alternative understanding of gaming and interactivity as contingent on user felt control. For Galloway, videogames less understood as dynamic conversations of users and systems and more as complex cybernetic assemblage of actions committed by both active human actors as well as autonomous machine operators.[13] Many of Galloway's examples include sequences such as cut scenes and loading screens, which for the author symbolize the latter and indicate their overwhelming presence in gameplay. *Dragon's Lair* specifically offers a productive case to think about the latter as the game is dominated by what Galloway calls non-diegetic machine operations—literally represented in the blanked and rolled buffering screens as the videodisc stylus resets—and diegetic machine operations—represented in the game's dense, evocative visual surface and animation—neither of which a user can directly "control," yet must experience in order to "play" the game.

Because of its lack of continuous control, *Dragon's Lair* necessitates that a user occupy both the position of film studies' spectator and game studies' player at the same time. Tellingly, some of the game's cabinets famously were equipped with two monitors: one below for the actual player and one above for people to gather and watch the game being played. Most of the game entails the user watching and examining visual information. This, in itself, is not entirely without precedent as many games from darts, to bowling, to golf include much more visual assessment than movement. And *Dragon's Lair* was released at a time when media theorists were re-assessing consumption and visual consumption specifically as a type of "activity," after decades of academic literature had denounced popular culture as the site of passivity and propaganda. Contemporaneous cultural studies researchers re-cast television viewership as a zone of struggle over meaning between encoders and decoders (Hall [1973] 2006; Eco 1989; Fiske 1987) and later cognitive theorist examined film viewing as an ongoing process of individual hypothesis creation and testing (Carroll [1990] 2015; Bordwell [1989] 2008). I argue that these trends can be addressed as a concomitant technological effect of a historically constrained means of media production beginning to thaw with consumer control devices like VCRs, videodiscs, and videogame consoles which, in essence, hacked and took control of television sets (itself a loaded term suggesting false stability). *Dragon's Lair* acts as an artifact and theoretical condensation of these debates as a new media control device that solicits a user to quickly and often critically assess filmic cues to advance through nodes and rooms. The visual world of *Dragon's Lair* is represented from a shifting, oblique, third-person perspective, unlike the flat plane perspective of then-contemporary arcade games that depicted single screen game worlds from above or to the side with no sense of a z-axis, unlike later "3D" games (beginning with titles like *Super Mario 64* (1996)) that mimed the earlier game's perspective but also gave users control of a virtual camera to depict the space. This combination of represented depth and fixed angle was the unique resource and limitation of *Dragon's Lair*'s laserdisc storage but also provided the game's specific technique of combining cues and actions. While rhythm games test users' tacit sense of musical conventions (playing on beat or in tune), Dyer's game tests users' tacit sense of film conventions such as angle, composition, off-screen space, screen location, and screen direction. In other words, while other contemporary game designers were integrating animation by allowing users to become de facto animators through avatar movement (see, e.g., Greenberg 2021), *Dragon's Lair*'s makers instead adapted the specific form of classical Hollywood animation as way to quiz users' visual intelligence.

In the first case, the game uses fixed camera angles to orient and disorient users. Each of *Dragon's Lair* rooms are made up of one or more filmed shots and many of these set-ups, with a handful of exceptions, have no virtual camera movement. Instead, the game uses fixed angles, which also simplifies animation work, both to cue a user on how to read the visual space and to respond to objects and environments. For example, in both the blacksmith's room and the haunted knight's room, the game's camera suddenly takes on high and distant of the view of the avatar, on the one hand, focusing visual attention and compositional, graphical space on an animated sword and ball-and-chain, and on the other hand, revealing the floor space which acts as a de facto maze indicating the correct directional path to escape the room (see fig. 1.7). In other words, a user must quickly process these extreme changes in angle choice and consider how the divergence is cueing pertinent visual information. Similarly, the game's shot selection also uses traditional optical point-of-view techniques from the implied perspective of Dirk to signal objects of mechanical

Figure 1.7   The Haunted Knight's Maze in *Dragon's Lair* (2017). *Source*: Screenshot Captured from the Digital Leisure PS4 Port.

importance—as in quick, subjectively loaded zooms into the sword needed to defeat the final boss dragon—of narrative importance—as in shots looking down the empty elevator shaft inflating Dirk's sense of vertigo—or libidinal importance—as in a series of close-ups of the captive princess, Daphne, a bald attempt at fusing the user's and the avatar's scopic drive. And in the very least, these point-of-view structures that cut into narrative space (typical in classical film form, atypical in videogames—until the innovation of first-person perspective (see Galloway 2006) inflate a sense of character and character desire at a moment when most games still primarily relied on abstract, extra-diegetic scoring for user drive and quasi-narrative motivation. Noel Burch (1986) makes similar claims about the transition from so-called primitive film to bourgeois film which cut into space and fuse spaces between shots, consequently helping to develop a sense of character psychology and a litany of accompanying ideological effects.

Conversely, these changes in fixed angle and presumed perspective also serve to disorient a user. For example, the elevator room in which a large platform falls beneath Dirk's feet is depicted in two consecutive top shots situated directly above the falling platform, in the first shot, and beneath the platform and attached it, in the second shot, as the elevator plummets straight down into the screen's z-axis. These shots from "above" strategically deny a user visual information of a lateral escape, but quickly the subsequent shot depicts Dirk on the platform in profile as a user must jump or move left or right, depending on the inversion. Here the use of a sharp camera angle divergence is designed conversely to deny the user the ability to pre-assess or measure their next move by blocking important visual information—no escape can be seen from above. Moreover, this short sequence also juxtaposes the two canonical perspectives of classic arcades—top down and side scroll—to create an interesting optical puzzle. And in all these cases, the use of fixed camera angles either prompts, or in interesting cases, occludes actions in an effort to vary game obstacles.

Rudolph Arnheim ([1941] 2011, [1969] 2015) in his works on art and visual perception has described the latter as a form of active, yet unarticulated intelligence. To demonstrate this concept, Arnheim discusses a series of hypothetical optical projects (images with blocked out portions, images with balanced or unbalanced compositions) in which images are often filled in or supplemented with the inferential work of observers, echoing E.H. Gombrich's (1959) "beholder's share." Arnheim also writes of assessments at work in the visual understanding of composition in which observers of two-dimensional imagery perceive the push and pull of balance as contents fill and empty out portions of graphic frames. Operationalizing this logic, many of *Dragon's Lair*'s obstacles amend narrative information (i.e., you have fallen into a trap) with visual compositional clues for their solution. Several rooms then feature obstacles in which moves are measured by scanning for and visually perceiving the film record's mise-en-scène for openings or compositional dead spots, soliciting a viewer's visual intelligence and ability to solve for graphic balance. For example, in the snakes' pool, a user is surrounded to the front (the top of the y-axis) and to one side (either extreme of the x-axis depending on the room's inversion). The only escape or solution is pushing the joystick to the unoccupied extreme of the x-axis. While this solution might seem self-evident, I argue that the correct move is based on both a particular image sense that detects and responds to compositional imbalance, and consequently disallows back or down on the joystick as an appropriate choice, as well as a filmic sense which also disallows back or down on the joystick as choice because of its contradiction to the forward/up screen direction, character orientation, and character movement of the room's previous shots. While fleeing or tag-like mechanics were very common to contemporary arcade games from *Frogger* (1981) to *Mappy* (1983) which are largely based avoiding advancing enemies and soliciting users to scan the playfield for openings for escape, I argue that *Dragon's Lair* is a unique variant of this pervasive form of gameplay in that it uses formal, graphic balance as a user resource (while, presumably, *Frogger* revels in its own visual chaos).

In Noel Burch's *Theory of Film Practice* (1973), the film theorist includes a chapter which describes every possible category of offscreen space, those hypothetical zones outside of a film image's frame lines with a fluctuating, hypothetical existence. This space may or may not exist at each of the four frame lines (top, bottom, left, and right) as well as behind the camera or recording instrument and far in the distance behind a set or any similar-serving obstruction. And, in Burch's estimation, it is up to the creative filmmaker to fully explore and complicate the shifting status of these narrative spatial zones. In a game of *Dragon's Lair*, the user themself must orchestrate this fluctuating existence through their movements and frame exits committed in response to nodes. To solve rooms, a user must often track offscreen space previously established in larger scaled shots, atypical at a time when most arcade games were still organized by single screens or looping screens per level (Wolf 1997). For example, avoiding the witch's spike thorns necessitates that a user jump off frame toward the graphic bottom, or down, to a safe zone seen in a prior larger frame, establishing shot of the room. Moreover, many of *Dragon's Lair*'s rooms necessitate movement into portals of undefined but pre-imagined offscreen space, and in a Burchian mode, the game solicits users to intermittently activate each; the graphic top or above frame as when Dirk is surrounded by snakes; the space beyond frame left as Dirk is swarmed by bats; and the space behind the set in the distant background as Dirk is trapped by tentacles. Much like early narrative film (see Gunning 1991), *Dragon's Lair* uses portals positioned at the frame lines or edges to stitch together onscreen and off-screen narrative space. And several rooms even solicit viewers to pre-figure off-screen space as a solution to nodes. In the Lizard King's room, a user must jump three times out into offscreen space behind a hypothetical set to avoid the mace blows of the enemy and retrieve Dirk's sword (see fig. 1.8). This later aspect contributes a confounding sense of chance and luck within the gameplay in which users are compelled to choose between

Figure 1.8   Lizard King Attack in *Dragon's Lair* (2017). *Source*: Screenshot Captured from the Digital Leisure PS4 Port.

equally unknown off-screen spaces—moving left down a blind hallway leads to death at the Lizard King's hands while the blind movement to the right leads to escape. Forced binaries like these recur in the teeter-totter room and the hurricane room where two plausible offscreen exits are presented but only one is correct.

Gaps between successive shots are likewise used to inform and complicate a user's understanding of screen direction in many of *Dragon's Lair*'s rooms. Screen direction, a conventionalized concept derived from film studies and the practice of filmmaking, maintains a sense of continuous space through the editing together of disparate shorts, or depicted sliced portions of time-space. It entails keeping a camera on one side of an actual or virtual set, commonly referred to as the 180° rule, and concomitantly ensuring that movement of objects in space through three-dimensional represented space continues on similar two-dimensional vectors in subsequent shots—a character moving from frame left to frame right or from frame bottom to frame top should be moving in roughly right-facing or upward directions in respective following shots. Either optically or culturally as an accepted form of visual grammar, this protocol theoretically reduces the disruption of each shot change. In the multi-shot rooms of *Dragon's Lair*, the game often uses this technique, reducing technological fissures of frame skipping. For example, in the oft-mentioned rope swinging room, the game presents seven shots filmed at roughly a perpendicular angle to the avatar's action as the user moves him from left to right or vice versa. Similarly, the snake pit room begins with an establishing shot that depicts the escape portal in the narrative back or screen top. And through six subsequent shots, with several changes in shot scale and angle, the escape remains located continuously at frame top. And in the longer rooms of the mechanical horse and the canoe rides the virtual camera likewise remains behind the avatar through a series of shots as Dirk, in each case, heads into frame along the z-axis, compelling a user to toggle the joystick left and right to avoid advancing obstacles. In all of these examples, *Dragon's Lair*'s use of screen direction creates a sense of spatial continuity through shots and gives the clues necessary to solve the game's optical puzzles.

Yet in several interesting rooms, the game manipulates and complicates a user's understanding of filmic spatial cues. In the slide room, Dirk enters through a door high in frame right and spots a sloping set of stairs below him culminating in a chasm with only a bridge at the extreme frame left offering him a passage through. The next shot looks over Dirk's shoulder moving the avatar to fill the left side of the frame and again depicting the lone bridge escape, but this time the bridge is now on the right side of the screen. Quickly shot three returns to the initial front-facing angle as all the stairs, save for those preceding the bridge retract, turning into a slide that will send Dirk to his death down the open pit. The trap itself is transparent enough—avoid the stairs that lead into a pit—but what makes the room difficult to master is the game's editing which shows the solution to the left, but then quickly moves to the right and then back to the graphic left (see figs. 1.9 and 1.10). Here the game tests a user's ability to construct mental narrative space outside and contradictory to traditional filmic construction. Similarly, the throne room quickly moves the avatar from frame edge right to frame edge left by way of a revolving door, forcing another rapid reassessment of spatial cues and escape lines. And, once again, in the witch's room, enchanted vines can only be avoided by combining a down and up keystroke in subsequent shots, even though the avatar is moving the same direction through multiple shots—it is the virtual camera which has shifted its space and a user's sense of spatial consistency.

Perhaps the best example of this technique can be observed in the boulder room (see figs. 1.11 and 1.12). In many ways the boulder room is a revision of the rope swing room (though vertically and not horizontally oriented) that solicits a set of consistently timed actions in a situation where possible moves and escapes are strategically limited.[14] The room depicts Dirk running from an enormous billiard ball in a parabola-shaped gully while avoiding a set of perpendicular boulders running along the gully's curve. Echoing the canonical shot from *Raiders of the Lost Ark* (1981), the room and its shots depict the principal ball coming down and outward along the z-axis, from the presumed background or frame top toward the user who must press the joystick down in time to avoid both the main boulder, as well as the cross-traffic of boulders moving from frame left to frame right, to escape through frame bottom. The room repeats this node four times, cycling the animation (again like the rope

Figure 1.9   Shot 1 of the Ramp Room in *Dragon's Lair* (2017). *Source*: Screenshot Captured from the Digital Leisure PS4 Port.

Figure 1.10   Shot 2 of the Ramp Room in *Dragon's Lair* (2017). *Source:* Screenshot Captured from the Digital Leisure PS4 Port.

Figure 1.11   First Shot of the Boulder Room in *Dragon's Lair* (2017). *Source:* Screenshot Captured from the Digital Leisure PS4 Port.

swing room), while only changing the color of the horizontally crossing ball. After establishing this vector moving down and away through four successive nodes and shots, the game suddenly places the virtual camera behind Dirk as a user must jump across another pit to escape the room for good and allow the chasing boulder to crash down. Or a user must press up on the joystick after visual cues and repetitive actions had conditioned them that "up" would

Figure 1.12   Final Shot of the Boulder Room in *Dragon's Lair* (2017). *Source*: Screenshot Captured from the Digital Leisure PS4 Port.

spell certain death and doom. Constrained, fixed framed shots accompanied with spatial continuity in these shots establishes a pattern of image and action which is confounded in the room's ultimate solution. In other words, interactivity in *Dragon's Lair* is not determined by continuous control or a lack of it but through visual activity which solicits a user to either keep track of spatial cues, or conversely, to read them critically. The appeal of such an experience was likely contingent on the relative richness of the game art which embedded these puzzles. This art of *Dragon's Lair* was created by Bluth, a late proponent of so-called full character animation who, for contextual reasons tracked in the next chapter, turned to the new medium of videogames, or what Bluth called "interactive movies," to practice his craft.

NOTES

1. Throughout the book, I will often use the term "videodisc" and not the more common descriptor, "laserdisc." Videodisc is the term that is found in the contemporary scientific literature and patent records (analyzed in chapter 3) to describe an entire class of invention and innovations, some executed and others not. Laserdisc refers to a specific, proprietary, trademarked use of digital disc media and is, therefore, the most theoretically general term to describe the plethora of media disc systems and uses at play at this moment.

2. Continuous audiovisual output, however, is not the same as continuous represented time of classical film narration, or even continuous gameplay, as examples of pause buttons, level breaks, and time-outs demonstrate.

3. To be sure, contemporary arcade games incorporated waiting in play—in *Track & Field* (1983) you must wait for the starter's gun and in *Popeye* (1983) you must wait for the branded theme song to end before collecting hearts—but in no other contemporary game is playing time so dominated by waiting as in the case of *Dragon's Lair*.

4. However, there is at least one last temporality important to acknowledge in all arcade games: service time. Players deposit credits to play a game for a constrained, terminable time, which could be very brief in particularly difficult and unforgiving game like *Dragon's Lair*. In her discussion of the economic subject positions of arcade game players, Carly Kocurek (2012) explains that the economic condition of the arcade acclimated players to a new, immaterial, predominantly service-based experience of the world. While I would argue that it is difficult to periodize market exchanges for terminable entertainment services (surely there are premodern precursors to these relations), I do agree that this economic window will be an important frame to consider in later chapters.

5. Greenwich Mean Time, for example, was only established in 1884, contemporaneous with other technological innovations based on and used to create, in Deleuze's formulation, a sense of any-time-whatsoever—a blank, standardized scientific notion of progressive time as an independent variable.

6. In fact, the construction of agency in *Dragon's Lair*'s cybernetic system echoes current post-capitalist concerns about the dismantling of traditional markers of work and meaning in technosocial systems overtaken by automation, replication, and artificial intelligence. In other words, not only are we the final input, often this input is superfluous.

7. Accepting conventional gaps like level breaks, vertical wrap-arounds in single screen games like *Pac-Man*, and unique mechanics like *Asteroids*'s (1979) "hyperspace," which, like a card game, re-shuffles the position of all screen objects.

8. The visual result of these might be described as a sensation of skipping.

9. This lack of control of the avatar and the space and any consequent feeling of a user's diminished power or agency was likely amended with the overt hypermasculinity of the screen content and story to be discussed more in chapter 4.

10. See also Bogost's (2015) excellent discussion of *Mirror's Edge* as a game that artfully includes a seemingly difficult and constrained control scheme.

11. If the object of chess is to capture the opponent's king, then why not just pick it up?

12. Of course, several games restrict user movement, but this restriction is often supplemented with the vicarious movement of bullets and projectiles as in *Space Invaders* (1978) (and all of its clones) as well as *Missile Command* (1980).

13. In this way, videogames act as a useful site to think about individual agency in technosocial systems more broadly. Indeed, the mixed critical legacy for *Dragon's Lair*, traced in chapter 3 must, in part, be attributed to the way the game complicates, and indirectly exposes, the promise of power and control which is central to the ideologically loaded promise of participating in so-called interactivity.

14. This room is the only other one that is discussed at length in Dyer's WIPO application.

Chapter 2

Dragon's Lair
The Business

The makers of *Dragon's Lair* assembled their work through a disorganized division of labor atypical of videogames at a time when production was still characterized by in-house, integrated producers who conceived, made, and manufactured arcade cabinets. Instead, the production had more in common with contemporary old media processes in film and television wherein specialties are dispersed across a number of focused firms who develop alliances for individual projects. Working at Mattel during the time of the first growth of electronic games, Richard Dyer devised a sword-and-sorcery game in 1977 that utilized an automatic paper scroll, similar to cash register tape, to cycle between narrative encounters (Robley and Kunkel 1984). But upon leaving Mattel in 1979, just as the market for electronic games was collapsing, Dyer and his new independent venture Advanced Microcomputers Systems (later renamed RDI Systems) pitched their invention to the fledgling animation house Don Bluth Productions as a prototype for a new videodisc game, a decision Dyer attributes to an epiphanic screening of *The Secret of NIMH* (1982).[1] Bluth and company organized between 50 and 70 of their staff on a 4- to 6-month production schedule to create 22 minutes of game footage (Brownstein 1984). Meanwhile, the El Cajon-based Cinematronics, a firm already struggling with a bankruptcy blamed on an overinvestment in vector-based graphic games and problems with cabinet counterfeiting, handled the eventual physical arcade cabinets (Skelly 2012). A contemporary magazine *Variety* in an article described the production of *Dragon's Lair* and its follow-up *Space Ace* stating,

> RDI employs a 25 person staff that scripts arcade games. Company artists draw out storyboards from which Bluth's artists perform the animation. RDI

engineers complete the programming and engineering of the games before Cinematronics takes over production and distribution. (Bierbaum 1984, 178)

And the costs of the unusually expensive game were shared by the three firms with Bluth Productions raising $1.2 million and RDI and Cinematronics contributing the remainder of the $3 million budget (Harmetz 1983). The three firms solidified their partnership as a domestic stock company, registering themselves as Magicom with the California Secretary of State on February 1, 1983, with Dyer as its lone named executive. In turn, Magicom filed trademark notices on the *Dragon's Lair* name in the U.S. Trademark office on August 26, 1983.

In this chapter, I offer a deeper examination of the media industries around *Dragon's Lair* and its principle makers, specifically tracking how uncertainty and volatility in the animation, film, and toy business along with the circumstances of the Video Game Crash, both structurally shaped and limited Bluth and Dyer's opportunities. Moreover, through this deep contextualization, I will demonstrate that the eventual fate, and even reputation of *Dragon's Lair*, along with its offspring the Halcyon, owes much to these forces as well as the larger push toward neoliberal enterprise and interactive subjects, both discussed at length in the final two chapters.

DON BLUTH AND FULL ANIMATION

In August 1982, the proprietors of the Rainbow Theater in Tujunga, California, received a message 2 days after they began to run a late summer double feature of Disney's *TRON* and Don Bluth Productions's *The Secret of NIMH*. In the message, a Disney-Buena Vista film rental representative notified the theater management that they would rather pull *TRON* from future screenings than have it play with *NIMH* and invoked the distributor's right to cancel a theater's contract in the case that a Disney film was to be exhibited with another feature that was "found to be of unsuitable character" (Caulfield 1982). The incident at the Rainbow Theater was repeated around the country as theater owners were sent similar missives, eventually invoking the ire of *NIMH*'s creator Bluth who claimed that he was preparing legal action against the Disney order adding that he "want[ed] to fight it like hell." The strange dust-up over the double bill appears as an odd incident—indeed what film could be of a more suitable character with regard to the Disney brand than Bluth's pastoral fable of good-natured and heroic rodents—but was symptomatic of industrial shifts and uncertainties in the business of American feature animation. Specifically, after years of diminishing film returns, Disney's *TRON* was a self-conscious attempt to broaden its brand and content beyond the confines of the children's cartoons that *NIMH* unapologetically emulated, and Bluth's fledgling animation outfit conversely was doubling down on the artistic and affective legacy of Disney's industrial and moral model. In other words, despite cosmetic similarities, both films represented radically different business logics and strategies to manage change. Moreover, the clash of Disney and Bluth was only the latest skirmish in a larger industrial and very public disagreement over the future of animation that had begun three years earlier in the so-called Disney Exodus or as one anonymous source at the time offered: "there is no question that Disney feels extremely bitter about Don Bluth."

On September 13, 1979, animation director Don Bluth offered his resignation to Disney Animation quickly prompting the exit of another two animating directors, four animators, six assistant animators, and one effects technician, all told equaling approximately one-fifth of the firm's total creative personnel ("Former Disney Animators . . ." 1979; "12 Animators Leave . . . " 1979; Goldrich, 1979). At the time, Bluth was a young animator who had worked on Disney's previous features *Winnie the Pooh and Tigger Too* (1974), *The Rescuers* (1977), and *Pete's Dragon* (1977) as the studio was retiring its longstanding creative workers, Disney's famed "Nine Old Men," animators whose credits extended back to the studio's first feature film, *Snow White and the Seven Dwarves* (1935) (Solomon 1982). And while the exact motivations and intentions behind this exodus are a matter of debate, the move certainly spoke to increasing contextual shifts and emerging opportunities in the larger media business as well as philosophical differences over the future of animation within it. As Bluth and company left Disney's Burbank lot, they merely moved down the street to a new Studio City office with a two-picture deal in hand from the new production shingle, Aurora Productions, itself headed by three expatriated Disney executives, first to adapt Robert C. O'Brien's *Mrs. Frisby and the Rats of NIMH* in 30 months using $30 million from "private investors" (Goldrich 1979; "Disney Exodus . . ." 1979, Dec. 21). This period was one of growth for several such mini-major and independent film deals, as firms like Robert Benjamin and Arthur Krim's Orion, Menahem Golan's Cannon, and Dino Di Laurentiis's DEG achieved mainstream theatrical success largely by leveraging increased and under-utilized demand for video cassettes and cable content as well as increasingly lucrative foreign distribution outlets to fund new productions. Although *NIMH* was financed with so-called private investors—or colloquially "dumb money"—Bluth seems very aware of these then-new media ventures and their potential. In a contemporary round table on the rationales behind the exodus, the animator flatly declared, "these new vehicles for full animation—disc and home entertainment— excite me" ("Disney Exodus . . ." 1979, 26). At this same event, an executive from Aurora Productions, James Stewart, further enthused that, "there is such a demand for film product today that one animation film every three years [the typical Disney production schedule] is hardly enough" ("Disney Exodus . . ." 1979, 26). And Stewart was not alone in his estimation and optimism for the field as 1983 promised to see the theatrical distribution of no less than ten animated features ("Bluth Completes Cartoon Feature," 1982).

Bluth also used the press coverage around the Disney Exodus to provide deeper rationales and justifications for the move, citing irreconcilable differences in the management and practices of animation labor. In the first case, Bluth espoused a single-vision philosophy of artistic creation and independence, casting Disney as a firm crippled conversely by groupthink as well as overt artistic and cultural conservatism. In an interview with the *Los Angeles Times*, Bluth explained that working at Disney "was a matter of constantly bumping up against Ron Miller [Disney president and later CEO] and the older guys who wouldn't relinquish authority and who wouldn't make decisions but by committee"; and later in conversation with the *New York Times*, Bluth offered, "[at Disney] the art of animation wasn't growing . . . the studio was so encrusted with its original and traditional ways" (Warga 1980; "Disney Attempts to Reverse . . ." 1981). Several years later, the animator also claimed that the conservative atmosphere created a workplace stifled by gender bias where it was difficult for women to advance, a claim anecdotally supported by the fact that 7 of the original 12 Bluth defectors were women (Harmetz 1984; Goldrich 1979). But even more frequently, Bluth spent time in the press not simply lauding the benign dictatorship of Walt Disney's firm but more so celebrating the founder's great belief in the laborious practice of so-called full animation. Briefly, full animation is a practice of cel animation most associated with the classical Hollywood studios and is distinguished by, among other things, its attention to visual detail, its meticulous rendering of individualized character movement, and its construction of illusionist depth effects (Sandler 2019). In Bluth's estimation, Disney had diminished these standards and practices. The animator delineated these principles in a public forum on animation stating,

> [Walt] perceived that characterization was of prime importance to the picture . . . characters need a great deal of dimension—not only in the way they move, but also in the way that they think, even in the way that they are colored. (Disney Exodus ... 1979, 31)

As such Bluth released his most damning critique in the press leading up to the release of his inaugural feature *NIMH* in which he claimed that he was told by Disney management not to spend time coloring the whites of eyes of figures in his work on the *The Rescuers*, an affront to the attention to visual detail Bluth claimed was the studio's hallmark (Mills 1982).[2]

The Disney Exodus created a bitter rift with Bluth's former employers that was only exacerbated by the amount of unflattering headlines created for Disney in the immediate aftermath: the *New York Times*'s "Wishing Upon a Falling Star at Disney" and *American Film*'s "Disney Looks for a Happy Ending to a Grim Fairy Tale" (Davis 1980; Mills 1982). According to contemporary press, the exodus resulted in a 6- month to a year-and-a-half production delay in Disney's subsequent animated feature *The Fox and the Hound* (1981) and created disorder in the firm's artistic personnel now left without a clear line of succession. As a result, both creative team and management at Disney used the press to respond to Bluth's claims and to further inflame the already acrimonious split. Longtime Disney animator Eric Larson chided Bluth and company stating, "they wouldn't accept responsibility . . . they were only interested in what they were doing outside the studio [and] they belittled everything that they were doing here" (Warga 1980, 36). And, with a bit more venom, Disney director of corporate communication Mike Spencer complained that

> if there was an oppressive atmosphere, Don Bluth created it. . . . I am amazed that when people are looking for an opposition view of the company they go to Bluth, a man whose only claim to fame . . . is that he walked out in the middle of a major production. (Davis 1980)

Additionally, a series of contemporary journalistic exposés analyzing the outward "failure" of leadership at Disney seemingly enflamed the animosity.

Released in summer 1982, *TRON* was a film engineered by Disney president Ron Miller and his young VP Tom Wilhite to answer many of the press's criticisms and to reconfigure the brand and corporate image of the company. Throughout the 1970s, Disney's film and television divisions languished, reaching a nadir in 1979 as film rentals contracted to only 4% of the domestic overall market, and film and TV revenue shrunk to 1/4th of the company's total portfolio (Davis 1980). Critics of this contraction diagnosed the problem as one of age and reputation. In the first case, Disney's "family friendly" brand created a boom period and was well coordinated with the demographic and larger cultural trends (suburbanization, neo-victorianism) associated with the Baby Boom and immediate post-WWII period, but as the birthrate declined "aging" the United States and cultural shifts associated with the so-called generation gap permeated, Disney did not respond. And while many of the original creative personnel of the firm's central animation unit aged out and retired, there was not a clear line of succession of new and equally productive talent.[3] Moreover, the Disney organization had also developed a reputation among agents and producers within Hollywood as only a "last resort" because of its refusal to give profit participation to its creatives (an increasingly common practice in the New Hollywood), its rejection of outside financing deals and its insistence on micromanaging creative decisions at the executive level—all tendencies that alienated young, creative talent (Warga 1980; Davis 1980; "Disney Attempts to Reverse . . ." 1981). *TRON*, in both its subject matter and its production, constituted an attempt by Disney management to address these shortcomings. In fact, the film's narrative literally depicts the attempt of young, innovative workers to fix a corporation from the inside out. In *TRON*, the protagonist, a videogame programmer Flynn, embodies a form of industrial wish fulfillment and enters the backend database of Endcom defeating the overbearing Master Control Protocol through a series of videogame contests. A story of gamified corporate reform, *TRON* transparently used the emerging narrative and visual vocabulary of videogames in an attempt to capture young audiences lost to Disney and concomitantly attracted to gaming, which was already doubling the annual gross of domestic theatrical box office ("Taking the Zing Out . . ." 1982). *TRON* also constituted an attempt by Disney to advance the age of its typical consumers, along with its adaptation of S. E. Hinton's young adult novel, *Tex* (1982) and its decision to continue work on an animated adaptation of Lloyd Alexander's fantasy novel *The Black Cauldron*, eventually released in 1985 at the end of the sword-and-sorcery revival described in chapter 4. In other words, *TRON* was copacetic with the firm's longstanding technique of branding strategy as programming invented and refined at Disney decades earlier and still in use today (Anderson 1994; Gillan 2015). To achieve the distinct look of the internal "game grid" of the narrative, Disney tapped outside creative talent including New York-based digital media firm MAGI (Mathematical Applications Group, Inc.), the French SF cartoonist Moebius (Jean Giraud), and the award-winning advertising firm Robert Abel & Associates. Insularity had been one of the chief criticisms of Disney under Ron Miller, however, *TRON* was symptomatic of a larger attempt by the studio to cultivate outside ties across the industry through co-productions, specifically with Paramount on *Pop-Eye* (1980) and *Dragonslayer* (1981), as well as with independent producers on Carroll Ballard's *Never Cry Wolf* (1983). However, the $20 million *TRON* failed financially upon release and fueled an ongoing battle between shareholders and family members, which ultimately resulted in the resignation of Miller and his replacement with Barry Diller's protegé Michael Eisner, a consummate industry insider.[4]

The Secret of NIMH, too, embodied its makers' vision for animation in both its construction and in its very theme. In the press following the Disney Exodus and the subsequent release of *NIMH*, Bluth made every attempt to espouse his belief in full animation and to connect his own work practice to classical animation by separating himself from his contemporaries—"right now everyone's trying to do [animation] on a shoestring budget and it keeps getting worse"—and connecting his own work back to Walt Disney—"we want to understand how [Disney] told stories and go from there" (Summers 1980; Warga 1980). And later Bluth offered, "we wanted to return to full classical animation and the only way to get that was by going out on our own" ("Branching Out . . ." 1982). These acts of public self-branding also constituted an attempt to shift the growing field of animation by pillorying the work of television based on limited animation, which Bluth character-ized as "just nothing" ("Disney Exodus . . ." 1979) and also by aligning himself with character-based animation versus the innovations of the more abstracted cartoon modern styles of another group of famous Disney defec-tors who formed the UPA Studios (Amidi 2006). Instead, Bluth's more tra-ditional philosophy of animation was based on depth, detail, and above all emotional identification that, as then-contemporary film theory suggested, could not be achieved through alienating, modernist-informed art or as Bluth himself put it:

> to hold an audience's attention for a feature length animated film you have to achieve identification—a catharsis for the viewer as you tell the story. The art-ist's presence must be removed, so that style does not intrude in this process of identification. You can't have the appearance of sketchy lines, paint marks or other reminders that it is not real, if you want to sustain interest. ("Bluth Completes . . ." 1982, 34).

And later, upon the release of *NIMH*, he added, "an audience can't identify with a drawing. Until we evolve a new style, we're stuck with the illustrative one" (Solomon 1982, 54). In other words, as *TRON* embodied Disney's small attempt to move into new forms of animation, *NIMH* conversely indicated Bluth and company digging their collective heels into the high classical, illustrative style and Disney-informed illusionism of animation history. And this classicalism also extended to Bluth's very business practice as his firm attempted to leverage the cute and affective connection of anthropomorphic character animation through aggressive licensing and merchandising deals, complete with a tour for Disneyesque life-sized puppets derived from *NIMH* (Auerbach 1982; [MGM/UA Ad] 1982).

Although an adaptation of an established, Caldecott award-winning children's novel, Bluth's *NIMH* presents a particular style and design that resonates with the fledgling firm's guiding principles as well as the founder's public gripes. If *TRON* can be understood as a narrative of corporate reform and innovation, then *NIMH* is just as clearly a fable about corporate decay and corruption. In the film, a group of super-intelligent rodents (popular imagery for Disney whose employees often refer to the company as the "mouse house") is led by a wise, but aged master who is increasingly aloof and disconnected (a clear enough Walt Disney analogue), and in this power vacuum pretenders and plotters attempt to wrest control of the rat colony. The film's central conflict revolves around whether the rodents should stay in their ancestral home living off power and electricity form an unaware farmer (a metaphor for the famous "Disney annuity" of a back catalogue of film properties that saved the firm from risk, and, in the estimation of many critics, prevented corporate risk-taking) or should they entrepreneurially start their own independent home in the wilderness. Obviously, the heroes of Bluth's film are those who espouse the latter. Thematically, the film was an attempt to "recapture the warmth, spirit and moral vision of early Disney features" (Summers 1980), ironically, by using the staid Disney narrative technique of placing children in peril, traceable through *Pinocchio* (1940), to *Dumbo* (1941), to *Bambi* (1942). In *NIMH* the protagonist Mrs. Brisby is fighting to move her house to save her desperately ill child. This narrative technique had already been used in Bluth Productions' try out short *Banjo, the Wood Pile Cat* (1979), which starred a lost kitten in the city, and later became the Bluth house style as *An American Tale* (1986), features the adventures of a lost child-mouse in late nineteenth-century New York City and *The Land Before Time* (1988) followed a group of young dinosaurs separated from their respective families, traipsing through a prehistoric wasteland and menaced by predators. And just as *TRON*'s new style and design can be understood as a re-branding effort by Disney, *NIMH* also acted as a calling card for both Bluth's young outfit and for full character animation more broadly. In the film, Bluth and his animators dutifully included many of the indicators that distinguish exemplary variants of this practice, incorporating richly detailed backgrounds, the movement of fluids, the representation of optical distortions, in addition to both the exaggerated physical performance of characters, best seen in the manic flapping movement of Jeremy the crow, and the emotionally loaded nuance of gesture, best seen in the grief-stricken protagonist Mrs. Frisby who moves in shrinking hunches throughout the film, snout perpetually cast down. Particularly important was the use of backlit animation to create the glowing, light-bleeding visual effect of the film's supernatural elements, and this technique subsequently became important in the creation of *Dragon's Lair*'s many flame and fire effects. In fact, *NIMH* could be read as a visual compendium of all that classical, full animation techniques can achieve (and were eventually deployed in the construction of *Dragon's Lair* as well). Therefore, the animosity between the backers of *TRON* and *NIMH* was overdetermined and was not solely the product of personal animus, but also became a metaphoric conflict for the future vision of both children's and animated film. Ironically, neither film was ultimately successful financially as both features were caught in the wake of the tremendous performance of Steven Spielberg's *E.T.* (1982), which quickly became the overall second

highest grossing film upon its initial theatrical release ("All Time Film Rental
. . ." 1983).

The financial failure of *NIMH* was, in part, a symptom of larger economic,
organizational and cultural changes in the film business that rendered Bluth's
model of full character animation increasingly difficult. Reportedly produced
from approximately $6.5 million of private financing along with another $4.2
raised for the film's prints and advertising, *NIMH* only managed to gross $12
million domestically in its first three weeks of release ("Bluth Hits Distrib
. . ." 1982). Likely little of this theatrical revenue would have returned to
Bluth Productions as a 17% take had been promised to distributor, United
Artists, as well as another 13% to Aurora Productions, which folded its
operations soon after the film's release (Tusher 1981; "Bluth Hits Distrib . . ."
1982). Moreover, the experience seemingly embittered Bluth himself who
subsequently lashed out at the film-going public, lamenting that the business
had "entered a world in which plot and character development [are] virtually
unimportant and the only emotions are those of a quick thrill" (Beckman
1983a, 26).

Beyond changing audience tastes, *NIMH*'s performance was likely
impacted by larger structural changes in the film business, exacerbated by
Bluth Productions' insistence on emulating traditional animation practice
in theme, style, and labor. Specifically, Bluth ignored the very public criticisms of contemporary Disney that had critiqued that studio's conservative
approach as the country grew demographically older. During the period of
the late 1970s and early 1980s, the quadrant-spanning model of the Lucas-
Spielberg blockbuster, with multiple appeals across age and (to a lesser
extent) genders, emerged as the new, successful business model. Moreover,
the aging of the animation labor force itself impacted Bluth's ability to produce. Commentators pointed to significant age and accompanying skills gaps
as the older workers, who staffed mid-century cartoon houses aged out or
retired. For example, a contemporary *New York Times* article cited declining
productivity rates for younger Disney animators, as the typical output for
worker on 1955's *Lady and the Tramp* was as high as five feet of footage
per week, while the same titled workers on 1985's long-gestating *The Black
Cauldron* managed only half or two-and-a-half feet per week (Harmetz
1984). Labor productivity and scarcity too impacted costs as limited animation for television became cheaper, averaging $400,000 per half hour, while
full animation like that produced by Bluth Productions cost well over $2 mil-
lion per half hour and Disney's *The Black Cauldron* was budgeted nearer to
$9 million per half hour ("Bluth, Cartoonist Settle..." 1982; Harmetz 1984).
The inherent cost and difficulty of full character animation also accelerated
as a result of a massive labor strike for animation workers commencing
immediately after the release of *NIMH*.

On August 3, 1982, IATSE 839, the union representing animators in Los Angeles County, went on strike, beginning an almost 3-month-long labor stoppage designed to coincide with the field's busiest season, production associated with the fall television schedule. Before the strike began, the union had issued a list of major grievances including increases to minimum wages, more liberal sick leave policies, and a change in how screen credits were allotted. However, by far the most contentious issue was the major animation studios' effort to remove the runaway production clause in the basic contract that prevented the studios from taking full advantage of international differential wages and global animators who would work for less than one-tenth of their U.S. counterparts. Most major animation studios had already taken advantage of this labor practice; in fact, by the time of the strike Hanna Barbera was sourcing two-thirds of its animation labor from Taiwan and Korea (Goldrich 1982). As the strike continued many smaller animation studios, like Richard Williams, Murakami & Wolf, Filmation, and Don Bluth, individually signed new, often more sympathetic contracts with the union; however, the larger studios like Disney and Hanna Barbera failed to capitulate ("Bluth, Cartoonist Settle . . ." 1982; Goldrich 1982; "Local 839 . . ." 1982). On October 13, 1982, the strikers broke ranks and went back to work with minimal concessions and no promise to curb runaway production, which Disney and Warner Brothers entirely eliminated from their contracts. The strike and its aftermath left Bluth, specifically, in a difficult position. Labor stoppages had shut down production on the firm's proposed next feature, *East of the Sun, West of the Moon*, and allowed financial partners to back out after having already spent $500,00 on the production ("Bluth, Cartoonist Settle . . ." 1982). Moreover, Bluth's deal with IATSE 839 inked before the strike's collapse left him in an uncompetitive position and, by 1985, the studio declared bankruptcy only to move across the San Fernando Valley under a different name and as a non-union shop. And, by the following year, Bluth, fully acceded to reigning business practice, de-camped and "ran away" with his entire operation to Ireland at a time when 80% of U.S. animation was being produced in East Asia ("Cartoonist Local . . ." 1982; "Bluth Relocating . . ." 1986).

Bluth and his collaborators had left Disney Studios with a definitive vision and philosophy, namely an overwhelming devotion to full character animation, but quickly the fledgling studio was besieged by structural challenges including demographic change, increasing costs, and evolving labor practices. To do the work they set for themselves, the studio had ballooned to a full-time staff of 65 workers who consumed a weekly operating budget of $50,000 ("Bluth Hits Distrib . . ." 1982; Beckerman 1983). But after the meager performance of *NIMH* and the collapse of *East of the Sun . . .*, Bluth Productions had a hard time luring investors or distributors to finance their second work (Beckerman 1983, July 15). Instead, they considered other avenues for the type of animation work that they produced; however, Bluth already and very publicly had demonstrated his disdain for animation for television and had worked hard to cultivate a brand identity contraposed to these limited forms, making typical cartoon ventures unviable for the new firm. Bluth found another venue in emerging new media, specifically videogames, which Bluth himself significantly dubbed "participatory movies" and which the animator cast as both a vehicle to finance feature animation, a "training ground for animators" to learn the meticulous art of full animation and an opportunity to train young eyeballs to appreciate it once more (Beckerman 1983; Arnold 1983). His firm's first effort in this new direction was *Dragon's Lair*. However, as Bluth himself reiterated in many of his contemporary interviews, the animator, by his own admission, had no idea how this game actually operated, an ignorance necessitating *Dragon's Lair*'s unique division of labor across media industries.

THE VIDEOGAME CRASH IN THE
FILM AND TOY BUSINESSES

Dragon's Lair, first displayed to the public at the 1983 Amusement Operator Expo in Chicago and subsequently appearing in videogame arcades later in July of the same year, arrived at an auspicious period in videogame history, commonly referred to as the videogame crash. Although much has been written on the causes and effects of this epoch-forming, industry-wide event (see Ernkvist 2008 and Wolf 2012), we un-controversially can mark it as a massive financial contraction of the business of videogames and a quick exit of formerly dominant firms, including most significantly the industry leading Atari. The crash also spanned the principal arms of the videogame business, both arcade, coin-operated machines and home consoles. At the beginning of 1981, pundits were lauding the explosive growth of these twinned businesses optimistically predicting a $16 billion annual market, citing a particularly successful 1980 when the industry outgrossed theatrical box office and cable TV combined (Crook 1982). But by the end of 1982, optimism in the press flipped into panic as total coin drop in the United States was almost halved from year to year, dropping from $7 billion to $5 billion ("Taking the Zing Out . . ." 1982), contributing to a shakeout of arcade operators over the subsequent year of approximately 60–70% (Arnold 1983) and a diminishment of overall arcade cabinet sales by one-third (Harris 1983). The crash, too, affected the home market for videogames as, in 1983, retailers reported sales being halved contributing to $536 million and $201 million respective losses at Atari and Mattel, the number one and two leading console manufacturers by unit sales (Kleinfield, 1983, Oct. 17). In the wake of this contraction, Atari's parent corporation, Warner Communications, sold its arcade division to Namco and its home console business to Jack Tramiel to the small price of $150 million ("Warner Unloads . . ." 1984).[5] And while the home market for videogames would regain its market share of entertainment dollars within the decade, the business of the videogame arcade in the United States never rebounded and continued to diminish. *Dragon's Lair* arrived in this competitive context and, armed with a definitive technological difference, using videodiscs to display its hand-drawn graphics—Bluth designed full animation sequences—and organizational innovation, positioning a deeper connection between old and new media producers, briefly found promotion by artists, pundits, and fans as a fix to the crash.

Additionally, the crash created concomitant impacts on adjacent and interconnected industries, specifically the film and toy businesses. In the former case, many of the Hollywood majors had attempted to stay abreast of new media change by either buying or partnering their way into early videogame production. As late as May 1983, *Variety* was highlighting these links—Gulf + Western's ownership of SEGA USA, Coca-Cola's purchase of Gottlieb-Mylstar, and Warner Communications' Atari's many studio connections—as fruitful in producing mutually beneficial projects and opportunities (Girard 1983). Despite voicing optimism around the laserdisc as a mechanism to share costs and popularity with traditional film, most of those responsible for these videogame-film industry partnerships dissolved these ties over the next year and a half: Gulf + Western, re-organizing after the death of Charlie Bludhorn, sold its SEGA holdings to pinball manufacturer Bally (Bierbaum 1983) and Columbia Pictures International sold off its videogame division, Mylstar, citing, in the words of executive Francis T. Vincent, "adverse market conditions and the persistent deterioration of the markets for our products" ("CPI Shuttering Mylstar . . ." 1984). These sell-offs and the strategic re-orientation they represented also highlight the resurgence of Hollywood's traditional business, namely domestic box office and film rentals that more than made up for the studios' relative failure in the new media business of videogames. As either a contributing cause, indicating either an absolute limit of U.S. leisure time and spending, or a windfall effect, benefiting from fleeing, frustrated videogame users, the performance of U.S. domestic box office greatly expanded in the years coinciding with the videogame crash. Specifically, in 1982 total box office expanded 16% from the previous year, reaching a record total of $3.45 billion (Murphy 1983), a record that was bested the following year by another 9% jumping to $3.77 billion ("A 1983 Chronology . . ." 1984). This growth was led by a new crop of high concept (Wyatt 1994) sequels, adaptations, and genre revisions, likely assuaged any worries over lost gaming quarters.[6] Moreover, the major film studios also found an easier and more successful way to sell their content in a new media format, namely in home video cassettes. Through the decade, sales of pre-recorded cassettes blossomed from $3.9 million in 1981 to $207.5 million in 1989 (Prince 2000, 95), and by 1990 home video revenue reached $14.9 billion, surpassing theatrical box office by $10 billion (Wasko 1994, 114). According to Frederick Wasser (2001), the amount of money made through home video fundamentally changed the film production economy by allowing major studios to overspend on budgets (including greatly inflating star salaries) as well as prints and advertising to the extent that producers could comfortably lose money in theatrical performance while still eventually returning a profit. This business practice significantly raised the barrier to entry for mini-major studios and entrepreneurial firms like Bluth's. More importantly, this uptick in traditional and new revenue streams coincided with and likely influenced the severing of ties with the videogames industry at precisely the time that *Dragon's Lair* was attempting such a gambit.

As theatrical box office was expanding, declines in videogames were also accompanied with an unexpected higher performance in traditional toy categories. Although toys and videogames are typically lumped together in business and trade reports, it was traditional toy firms who, increasingly like the film studios, distanced themselves from videogames and re-energized legacy lines like dolls and action figures and, thereby, enjoyed the spoils of demographic and industrial shifts in the field. In the late 1970s, many toy firms, thanks to the reduced cost of microprocessors, pursued a brand new market with successfully selling electronic devices such as Mattel's *Electronic Football* (1977) and Milton Bradley's *Simon* (1978).[7] However, just as quickly as this market developed, it contracted and was replaced with emerging console gaming; in 1976, the electronic games market accounted for $550 million in toy sales, or approximately 10% of the industry, only to collapse to $300 million in 1981 resulting in a massive glut of product (Salmans 1981). Many in the field turned next to the model of console gaming provided by Atari's VCS with Mattel's Intelivision (1979), Coleco's Colecovision (1982), and Milton Bradley's Vectrex (1983), and even Parker Brothers briefly entered the market as a third-party developer of console games. But with the eventual collapse of all four of these systems, the toy business, counterintuitively, grew, and industry focus and consumer spending resorted to other product lines. This expansion can partially be credited to demographic shifts in the U.S. as the country underwent a small "baby boomlet," as baby boomers increasingly graduated to childrearing and consequently floated toy sales. For example, in 1982 there were 37 million births in the United States, and more importantly 43% of these children were first born thus introducing approximately 16 million new potential customers to the toy sector (Sanger 1983). In this period as the mood of high 1980s consumption and materialism ascended, the toy industry massively grew from a $6.3 billion market in 1981 to a reported $12 billion in 1985 (Salmans 1981; Gutis 1985). This surprising growth made the toy segment one of the highest performing in the entire U.S. economy with industry leaders Coleco, Hasbro, Tonka, and Mattel boasting 59.3% stock increases in 1985 while the previous year toy earnings overall had doubled (Vartan 1985). Strategy in the field changed with attempts to move toys away from the seasonal nature of the past business by replacing one-off objects with collectible and expandable product lines, by introducing product launches throughout the calendar year, and by dispersing advertising spending more liberally throughout the financial quarters while still mostly focusing on Q4 (Gutis 1985).[8] Additionally, toy companies also developed strategic alliances with smaller, limited animation studios such as Marvel and Ruby-Spears who tapped inexpensive East Asian drawing labor—exactly the type of competition that had rallied the abortive IATSE 839 strike—to produce half-hour cartoon series around their products and using the limited animation techniques demonized by Bluth and his cohort, effectively creating branded entertainment and serialized advertising for a growing youth audience. And all these new cartoon series found welcome homes on the expanding television dial currently augmented by Reagan's FCC's expansion of the media system through the deregulation of station licenses (Caves 2005) along with contemporary growth of cable systems and their own inflating station carriage.

So, as videogames crashed, toys were booming; the changing fortunes of several leading firms help to tease out this nuance. As stated earlier, the expansion of the toy business was inconsistent over industry subsegments, and one of the best performers was traditional toys and dolls and action figures specifically, which expanded by 20% from 1982 to 1983 as electronic and videogames collapsed (Hollie 1984). El Segundo-based Mattel had been a pioneer in electronic games and console gaming, but after the collapse of Intellivision, the firm had divested of "everything but its traditional operations," that is Barbie dolls, Hot Wheels model cars and Masters of the Universe action figures (Hollie 1984). The last of these was a significant success for the firm, selling 125 million units of the sword-and-sorcery-themed product in the year of its launch (1982) and eventually grossing $1 billion in toys and licensing by 1985 (Stevenson 1985). Conversely, the firm Hasbro never participated in electronic or videogames and seemingly prospered for it. In the year of the videogame crash (1982), the firm posted $7 million in profits, buoyed by the $100 million in sales of their new re-launched action figure line G.I. Joe (Hassenfield 1985). This success, in fact, lured Warner Communications' Steven Ross—whose firm was experiencing the reversed fortunes of the videogame business—who oversaw a 40% stake purchase of the traditional toy manufacturer ("Sale of Knickerbocker . . ." 1982).

Meanwhile, Nolan Bushnell, Atari's original founder had, by 1986, divested himself of all his business ventures, save Axlon, a firm focused on bringing robotic and animatronic toys to the market (Edwards 2017). By 1984, Hasbro was able to purchase its ailing competitor, Milton Bradley, for $350 million, and by 1985 the firm's two principal product lines, G.I. Joe and Transformers, both accompanied by Marvel-produced animated television series, accounted for nearly one-fifth of all U.S. toy purchases (Jones 1984; Hassenfield 1985).

But no firm's biography indicated the shifting fortunes of the industry better than that of Coleco. The ambitious leatherworking and fiberglass pool concern produced the successful Colecovision videogame console in 1982, and, in the year of its launch the console accounted for 70% of the firm's sales (Duffy 1983). Coleco used this success to attempt to transition into the home computer market with their Adam computer, a plan which included purchasing the home license for *Dragon's Lair* for $2 million and a partnership with Pioneer and Philips to create a peripheral laserdisc player to make the game technically feasible (Bierbaum 1983; "Coleco Looks . . ." 1983). Further, Coleco even promised *Dragon's Lair*'s publisher, Magicom, $250,000 first sale home rights on all their future laserdisc titles (Bierbaum 1984). The Adam, plagued with chronic underproduction, unit failures, and marketing overpromises fizzled at launch, but Coleco was supported by another product launch that same year: Cabbage Patch Dolls. The Cabbage Patch line was introduced in June 1983, just before the Adam computer slowly trickled into stores, and it was immediate success. In the following year the line grossed $540 million in sales and by 1985 the dolls accounted for 75% of the firm's total sales (Kleinfield 1985, July 21).

The shifting fortunes of these firms demonstrate a fissure in toy and videogame manufacturing. All three—Mattel, Hasbro, and Coleco—moved to a strategy of exploiting traditional toy products and branded them across an expanding line of products and tied them into old media and its expanding, cluttered channel space. And just as the film studios were scurried away from the diminishing performance of videogames and were sympathetically lured by massive gains in VHS and box office, so too did the toy industry entirely readjust to a higher performing segment, notably leaving videogames to computer and electronics firms. All of this, too, may have been influenced my macroeconomic turmoil related to the U.S. recession of the early 1980s, which may have dissuaded speculative long-term investment in new media, but certainly would have shrunk consumer interest as unemployment grew to 10.8% nationally in November 1982 according to the U.S. Bureau of Labor Statistics, a number considerably higher in traditional manufacturing regions like Michigan where unemployment spiked to 16.5% in the same period. And, all things being equal, dolls are much less expensive to develop, produce, market, and sell than videogames. *Dragon's Lair* was released amidst these shirting economic realities and industrial priorities.

DRAGON'S LAIR AND THE "LAZER CRAZE"

By most measures, both financial and critical, *Dragon's Lair* was an immediate success. After a brief test run at the Amusement Operators' Expo, Magicom released the game on June 23, 1983, and, in response, several newspapers recorded pieces bragging of long lines and intense interest at local arcades. One such piece claimed that the game was twice as profitable as typical arcade cabinets, returning a storefront's investment in only 4 weeks and that the game's very presence had increased arcade foot traffic by 25–50% (Bierbaum 1983). Cabinet sales too were robust; by January 1984 Magicom had sold approximately 8500 units at $4000 a piece, twice the price of traditional arcade cabinets (Harmetz 1984). Although the sales were lower than the optimistic projects, of 100,000 units, a figure that would have rivaled *Pac-Man*'s (1980) popularity, *Dragon's Lair* was seemingly hindered by the sheer lack of commercial laserdisc players and the limited production capacity for this necessary component in the United States (Harmetz 1983). In fact, one contemporary magazine article estimated that there were only 100,000 total laserdisc players in the entire U.S. 6 months after the game's release (Hurwood 1983). Nonetheless, in response to the immediate buzz and returns around the game, Bluth announced a new and ambitious business plan of producing five similar "movie games" a year and to sell the new games to existing Magicom cabinets on a release and re-release schedule not dissimilar to film rentals, but also echoing the archival re-release techniques pioneered by Disney's distribution arm, Buena Vista (Harmetz 1983; Brownstein 1984). Moreover, both business pundits, technology reporters, and even early videogame critics heaped praise on the game. A writer at *Backstage* pointed to the game as a way to save the failing animation industry (Beckerman 1983). A reporter from *Infoworld* singled the game out stating, "the videogame industry is truly dead, double laserdisk games like *Dragon's Lair* notwithstanding" (Gantz 1984, 20). And even though subsequent released videodisc games would often fare poorly in the estimation of emerging game critics, *Dragon's Lair* continued to be the one shining example and measuring stick by which all attempts would be gauged ("Play Now . . ." 1984; Bloom 1984).

This early success also excited exploitation in other media. Several licensed products based on *Dragon's Lair* were produced: a trading card set from Fleer, a lunch box from Alladin, and a board game produced by Milton Bradley. Additionally, the animation studio Ruby-Spears produced a short-lived half-hour animated series based on the game for ABC. Ruby-Spears, a cartoon studio specializing in limited animation for television founded by two former writers for Hanna Barbera, had already attempted to leverage videogame properties into television with the previous year's *Saturday Superarcade*, an omnibus program featuring animated shorts starring, among others Exidy's Q-Bert, Activision's Pitfall Harry as well as Bluth and Dyer's follow-up Space Ace (Perlmutter 2014). From these original properties, Ruby-Spears incorporated the rough visual design, settings, and conflicts from the original games, but in many cases the abstraction of the source material necessitated substantial elaboration. For example, the show bible for the Q-Bert segments evidenced conceptual expansion and confusion with regard to how to adapt the simple puzzle-pursuit arcade experience in terms of narrative conflict—the show is described as "about teenagers involved in teen conflicts"—in terms of character exposition—Q-Bert is pitched as a "combination of John Ritter (*Three's Company*) and Tony Curtis"—and even in terms of visual design, as early concept drawings show indecision around whether Q-Bert's extended snout is a mouth or a nose (Greenfield 1983). What this production document indicates is that, given the narrative and visual sparseness of most early videogames, adaptations often incorporated other elements borrowed across film and television; indeed, the Q-Bert document is filled with kaleidoscopic references to Goldie Hawn, Eddie Haskell, Dobie Gillis, and Lenny & Squiggy, all to make sense of the game sprite. Conversely, the problem of abstraction worked in the opposite direction with *Dragon's Lair*, which because of its construction was complete with clear conflict, character motivation, and visual design. Instead, Ruby-Spears, to accommodate the cost and speed of television work, simplified the art using limited animation techniques, precisely the style that Bluth's work, including *Dragon's Lair*, was designed to evangelize against. This abstraction of design and simplification of processes with respect to the original game demonstrates the economic realities of animation work and the competitive state of branded children's entertainment that was increasingly reliant on cross-platform properties from videogames, comic books, films, and increasingly dolls and action figures.

Also, *Dragon's Lair*'s success at the arcade helped to spark a short-lived trend of laserdisc videogames. At the annual Amusement Machine Operators' Expo in 1984, one year after the premiere of *Dragon's Lair*, no fewer than 13 laserdisc games were on display, including games from many major publishers such as Mylstar's *Mach 3*, Stern's *Cliffhanger*, and Williams's *Star Rider* as well as games from less conventional sources such as *CubeQuest*, created with contributions from the award-winning advertising firm Robert Abel & Associates ("Play Now . . ." 1984). The initial excitement for videodisc games, too, was undergirded by the increasing industrial discourse and technological experimentation around so-called interactive media, discussed more in chapter 3. Moreover, the new format likely garnered overheated interest based on the possibility of implementing easy convertibility to pre-bought machines in a time of the rapidly changing fortunes of arcade owners. The trend was also covered extensively in journalistic and popular criticism, yet, was ultimately very short-lived, simply recapitulating in microcosm to the boom-bust structure that had plagued both electronic and videogames more broadly.

Even though both *Dragon's Lair* and its SF-themed follow-up *Space Ace* enjoyed immediate financial and critical success—in fact *Space Ace* sold 1500 cabinets in its first week in release—the so-called laser craze subsided quickly (Crook 1984a). Lay persons' history of videogames often attributes the success and longevity of games, game types, and game makers to some judged superior quality, posing the progression of the medium as an evolutionary system based on competition and survival of the fittest. According to such a model, videodisc games would be considered a novelty but ultimately an inferior platform occupied by uninspired opportunists. But quality is a sociocultural term, debated and negotiated by interested parties, and not inherently residing in the substance of the game itself as either a physical object or a textual experience. Participating in an emerging discourse on interactivity, many critics attacked the flood of 1984 laserdisc games as empty iterations of previous titles, or as one critic put it, "nearly all the laserdisc games feature retreads of familiar game concepts like *Tempest* or even *Space Invaders*, played out with the usual computer-generated figures, against a backdrop of gorgeous 'wallpaper'" ("Play Now . . ." 1984). Similar negative assessments, along with rapidly changing expectations of electronic media and a retrospective historical gaze at the medium that, because of technological churn, picks clear winners and losers and has clouded many of the structural, technological, and cultural factors influencing the rapid rise and seemingly quick decline of the videodisc game. But one other clear, practical factor concerns *Dragon's Lair*'s inflated budget and its access to other markets.

Dragon's Lair was an expensive game to produce, costing approximately $3 million, or between two and four times as much as other contemporary games (Winslow 1984). And, as the arcade business hemorrhaged, impacted by financial contraction as well as the push toward social regulation by local municipalities eager to invent codes and restrictions to disperse the congregating teenagers that arcades attracted, expensive games necessitated multiple markets to ensure viability. This echoes the manner in which contemporary high concept blockbusters from Hollywood were predicated on the expanded markets for content on home video, cable, and increasingly important overseas film rentals. More specifically, games needed a home version (and perhaps even a lunchbox); however, the laserdisc format itself languished in adoption rates. Limited production capacity of players negatively impacted the manufacturing ability of game producers and limited consumer interest keeping the market for the format and small niche. As mentioned earlier, when Coleco purchased the license to produce the home version of *Dragon's Lair*, the firm had planned to produce an optical drive to work in concert with their new Adam computer ("Coleco Looks . . ." 1983). But when the technology never emerged, Coleco released a drastically modified version of the game that abstracted the look of the original title and added platforming mechanics into the gameplay. Keenly aware of this problem, Dyer also attempted to manufacture his own home laserdisc system, the RDI Halcyon. In other words, I conjecture that the fate of videodisc games was tied to the inability of optical media to enter the home market in the 1980s more than any fault of the games or their makers. Of course, videodiscs specifically and optical media in general did eventually become ubiquitous in U.S. homes in the subsequent decade in the form of CDs, CD-ROMs, and DVDs, but only after it was re-branded as "multimedia."

THE AFTER-LIFE OF *DRAGON'S LAIR* AND THE LURE OF COMPUTERIZATION

After years of being strictly a hobbyist's pursuit, several so-called turnkey mini-computers were brought to market in the late 1970s that were both pre-assembled (unlike, for example, the piecemealed Apple I) and featured graphical output, or colloquially graphics. As a new product category, these early home computers had a high degree of "interpretive flexibility" (Newman 2017), but a large portion of the pitch for these devices positioned them as game-playing machines. And this new focus on form and function placed videogame producers, familiar with both graphical output and game design, as the ideal entrants into this new retail space. In part informed by the refinement of cheaper silicon microprocessors, the new push toward computers answered a new socially widespread desire for the devices and specifically the industrial push to foment, exploit, and expand this desire. Computers, as new miracle devices, redundantly appeared in popular print media, on magazine covers, in think pieces, and across popular culture, and were even featured as narrative plot hooks and as characters in their own right. Also, a rash of influential, futurist business books such as John Naisbitt's *Megatrends* (1982), published by Atari's parent company WCI, and Alvin Topfler's *Third Wave* (1980) cast near-future scenarios of the U.S. home and workplace completely altered by the computer. As Topfler divined, "small cheap machines, no longer requiring a specifically trained computer priesthood will soon be as omnipresent as the typewriter . . . home computers will soon be selling for a little less than a television set" (185). And while the McLuhan-influenced arch-conservative

Topfler was ultimately more interested in containing and directing broader cultural presumed "effects" of the computer on our human institutions and subjectivity, business treatises like *Megatrends* worked more to excite a gold rush, pointing to inflating sales and productivity figures, for example pointing to the number of computer retailers in the United States growing from 50 total in 1977 to 10,000 in 1982—becoming a new, low-cost media storefront sandwiched between shuttering arcades and blossoming video rental houses (25). Similarly, this rush to the home computer was also underwritten by no less an authority than the United States International Trade Commission who, in 1984, authored a competitive trade assessment to examine the overall contraction of the videogame business (USITC 1984). In the report's key takeaways, the collective author suggested that laserdisc games may staunch the losses in the arcade field but looked to computers as the logical future of the field, flatly stating, "only the videogame manufacturers which are successful at marketing home computers are expected to survive the merger of videogame systems and home computer markets. Similarly, game cartridge manufacturers must explore applications programs [*sic*] to maintain their reputation and marketability" (XIV). In other words, the contraction of videogame sales contributed to a growing popular and industrial common sense that forecast the future of games in computers and the likely victors of this new field as former game makers.[9] This logic clearly swayed industry leaders at Atari, Coleco as well as *Dragon's Lair*'s creator, Rick Dyer.

So, as the crash continued in the American market, domestic firms reached out to the computer business. An early adapter, Atari released its first minicomputer models, the 400 and the 800, as early as 1979. And when WCI sold the struggling division to former Commodore executive Jack Tramiel, the firm refocused its efforts on home computing, releasing the ST computer line in 1985. In 1982, Arnold Greenberg's Coleco announced the imminent release of their own home computer, the aforementioned Adam, which was plagued with production problems. The firm only produced 100,000 and not the 500,000 units that it had promised by the end of 1983, and one contemporary news article cites unit return rates as high as 60%, a problem probably only exacerbated by Coleco's decision to outsource customer support (Duffy 1983). Despite the limited success of his peers, Dyer, too, attempted to pivot his success with *Dragon's Lair* and Magicom into hardware manufacturing. After reportedly spending $5 million on research & development, Dyer announced the 1984 product launch of the Halcyon, a natural language—that is, it could be operated with speech—laserdisc-based home computer and videogame machine (Crook 1984b). In promotional coverage in advance of the product launch, Dyer discursively recategorized *Dragon's Lair* from an arcade game to a computer technology stating, "I always planned to make a highly intelligent home computer system . . . *Dragon's Lair* was a test to see how this type of technology is received" (Zuckerman 1984, 29). And for this system, Dyer's RDI produced yet another sword-and-sorcery game with hand-drawn art assets. However, this game dramatically expanded the limited choice palette binary decision model by switching the input interface from an 8-directional joystick and single button, the iconic physical interface of arcade gaming, to a microphone headset and a 37-button keyboard, the last of which had already become a standard interface for emerging microcomputers (see fig. 1.5). The game, *Thayer's Quest* (1984), similar in setting to *Dragon's Lair*, featured distinctly different art as RDI collaborated not with Bluth Productions, but with the limited animation firm Murikami, Wolff & Swanson who specialized in children's television cartoons. Despite the significant investment, the Halcyon, like all competing attempts by U.S. videogame manufacturers never received widespread adoption; in fact, there is still considerable debate among hobbyist historians as to whether the product was ever really commercially available to consumers or if the units that exist today were simply for demonstration purposes.

Strategically, Dyer's Halcyon participated in the rush toward computerization and did so by aligning the device both discursively and technologically with optical lasers and natural language, both of which would have marked the unit as bleeding edge in 1984. In the case of the later, discourses on computer advancement from the Turing test to Hal's impassive monotone, position human-computer conversation as a pinnacle in sophistication. Natural language specifically recurs in contemporary business literature around computerization and is touted by writers like Topfler who pointed out that "voice data entry terminals in existence today are already capable of recognizing and responding to a vocabulary of one-thousand words . . . [and firms] are racing to expand that vocabulary, simplify the technology and radically slash the costs," constituting nothing less than the reconsideration of the very concept of literacy (188–89). The Halcyon existed at the vertex of these discussions; unfortunately, during a fateful appearance on the Bay Area's local TV program *The Computer Chronicles* from March 26, 1985, the device failed to recognize and respond to the voice commands of its creator (see fig. 2.1).[10] Yet there is a great historical irony in the failure of the system that prefigures current media trends, which recuperated its ideas, be they recategorized, reconceptualized, and rebranded. Of course, home computing systems would populate American homes and merge with old media devices. And over the next decade, videodisc systems did indeed become ubiquitous. And, lastly, natural language computing, now re-branded as part of so-called machine learning, continues to be an asymptotic ideal of interface innovators, as evidenced more recently in Google's 2018 ballyhooed presentation of the Duplex assist technology which seemed to allow an interlocutor to converse seamlessly with a virtual being to arrange for a hairstyling appointment over

Figure 2.1   Rick Dyer with the Halcyon Appearing on the *Computer Chronicles* (January 14, 1985). *Source:* Screenshot by Author.

the phone—really just a re-do of Dyer's previous demonstration and for a more prosaic function.[11] In short, the Halcyon's ultimate failure may be less interesting than the way in which the system demonstrates the recurrence of unrealized technological desires cross-referenced with discursive realities and industrial practicalities of the moment. In the next chapter, I will investigate more deeply each of these contexts by broadening the analysis to incorporate the growth of the concept of interactivity itself as well as the entrepreneurial efforts of several media makers who, like Bluth and Dyer, attempted to take advantage of its perceived potentials.

Indeed, the mixed legacy of *Dragon's Lair* seems quite different when all these contextual factors are taken into account. Shifts in the business of film and animation lured Bluth into game making at precisely the moment that they were losing major film studio support and traditional animation collapsed as a business. Likewise, shifts in the toy business prompted Dyer into game making at precisely the time that mainstream makers pulled up stakes and refocused efforts on dolls celebrated by inexpensive half-hour television commercials disguised as programming. And while home computing loomed as a solution to expand and refine the production and business model of *Dragon's Lair*, untested markets and technology complicated Dyer's subsequent efforts. The game's supposed failure then instead serves as a vital historical lens suggesting to investigate changing priorities and industrial uncertainties in the then-still-emerging business of videogames, or in the words of technology historian Kenneth Lipartito, "failures are not inherent in hardware but constructed by contingent social conditions" (52).

NOTES

1. During Dyer's tenure at Mattel, the toy firm also produced several electronic games around sword-and-sorcery themes similar to Dyer's invention, specifically two games licensed the emerging sword-and-sorcery gaming brand, *Dungeons & Dragons*.

2. Indeed, the 1970s do seem to be a period of increased artistic shortcuts in drawing labor at Disney as evidenced in recent video essays detailing the amount of reuse or swiping of animation from previous features.

3. Notably many of the older workers came to the studio in the staff increases that began in 1935 to begin work on *Snow White* and were lured by a national search for creative workers at a time when artistic labor was still hard to come by. And, as a result, fledgling animators and artists (including Carl Barks and Walt Kelly), moved across the country for the opportunity (Barrier, 2015). In other words, the labor-intensive practice of full animation likely was made possible by a desperate and willing source of docile labor.

4. While Eisner and his corporate "Team Disney" (J. Katzenberg and W. Mechanic) receive much of the credit for re-creating contemporary Disney (see Wasko 2001), many of the successful pillars of their strategy—focusing on cable TV, exploiting home video, creating a more "adult" line of feature films, and revitalizing feature animation—pre-existed in nascent form, all be they less successful during Ron Miller's tenure (Mills 1982; Harmetz 1984).

5. This later sale led to a series of stock holder lawsuits against Warner ("Warners Communications Sets . . ." 1985).

6. However, in the second half of the decade, U.S. box office did suffer another contraction before another period of tremendous growth in the 1990s.

7. Videogame innovator Ralph Baer co-created the prototype for *Simon*.

8. This strategy of expanding product lines notably presages the franchising and branding techniques of most major contemporary cultural industries.

9. The overheated interest in computerization among U.S. videogame makers also contributed to geographic shifts in the industry moving the center of the video-game business toward Japan and East Asia, a resorting with consequences that exist to this day.

10. The episode is viewable at https://archive.org/details/Lasersan1985

11. As of this writing Duplex still exists, but only as a method to facilitate services reservations—outwardly a rather limited application of such a sophisticated piece of technology.

Chapter 3

Dragon's Lair

The Disc

Upon the 1982 opening of Walt Disney World's EPCOT Center, visitors could find, just beyond the park's signature geodesic sphere Spaceship Earth, a bank of touch-responsive video monitors dubbed the Worldkey Information Service.[1] From these monitors, visitors could access audio and video information describing the new amusement park's features by clicking on an animated graphic map, constituting a virtual navigation superimposed on the already-simulated space of the park. Beside the Worldkey was a building called a Communicore which housed several other touchscreens called Interactive Entertainment Displays (IEDs). These displays housed games meant to highlight then-cutting-edge communication technologies: "Network Control" depicted the complexity of modern message distribution; "Phraser" highlighted the use of speech synthesis; and "Lost for Words" deployed advanced speech recognition.[2] Charles Leland, a liaison between the exhibit's corporate sponsor Bell Labs and Disney, bragged of the IEDs' hall stating, "it uses videodiscs to provide realistic, full motion video scenes that are far more sophisticated than the computer graphics and text displays of your typical arcade games" (Morningstar 1983, 29). All of these gadgets fit right into EPCOT's twinned themes of progress and promise, both of which were often measured in developments in information processing. The philosophy is graphically depicted in Carlo Mazzoli's mural adorning the side of Spaceship Earth (see fig. 3.1). On this image's bottom is a prehistoric cave dweller scrawling a crude image of a mastodon on a rock wall, and the composition extends diagonally, upward to two superimposed astronauts in spacewalk working on an orbiting satellite. Here the simple technique of iconic mark-making naturally ascends to contemporary global communications. Contemporary press touted the park as a showcase for technological prototypes for the utopian devices of the

Figure 3.1   Claudio Mazzoli's Mural for Spaceship Earth (1982). *Source*: Photo by author.

near future, indeed the Worldkey was the first working ARIEL (Automatic Retrieval of Electronic Information) system created by Bell, who had designs for its placement in public places across the United States (Fjellmen 1992, 378). But we can also look at the park as a prototype for a different relationship to technology for both media industries and media consumers, and interested parties often projected this change on the very public promise of the videodisc, the central component to the Worldkey, the IEDs, and to *Dragon's Lair*.

In this chapter, we will investigate the videodisc itself, focusing less on how the recording medium works and more on how it was understood by inventors, business leaders, and dreamers, contributing to what we can call the interactive imagination. During the late 1970s and early 1980s, interactivity, at best a fuzzy concept, itself emerged as a guiding topoi for media technology. Media archeologist Erkki Huhtamo (1997) used the term topoi as an analytic unit describing the historical recurrence of motives, desires, and meanings in discourse traceable in chronologies of invention. Huhtamo goes as far as to suggest that media history itself "lies primarily in the discourses that guide and mold its development, rather than in 'things' or 'artifacts' that . . . form the core around which everything (r)evolves" (222). Here I will position *Dragon's Lair*, along with EPCOT's prototypes as well as many other proposed and executed interactive TV and videodisc experiments, as a topoi, as condensations of discourse generating and perpetuating dreams of interactivity.

I have begun with a brief description of EPCOT because its use of the videodisc and its specific embodiment of interactivity prefigure the themes of sluggish institutions and re-conceived subject positions that recur throughout this chapter's brief historical sketch. Although Disney workers initially conceptualized EPCOT as a living, working community, its eventual construction took shape as a World's Fair-styled exhibit place where deep-pocketed sponsors, such as General Electric, General Motors, and Kraft Foods, among others, financed individual show pavilions and attractions. Participation offered these firms the opportunity to tell enormous crowds hopeful, future-directed stories combining an embrace of new technologies as a redemptive force with old fashioned ballyhoo, or, more pointedly, in the words of Disney imagineer Marty Sklar, "[i]ndustry has lost credibility with the public, the government has lost credibility, but people still have faith in Mickey Mouse and Donald Duck" (Allen 1982, 43). Further, like Disney's previously described foray with *TRON*, EPCOT itself too can be understood as part of the firm's attempt to update its brand image and age its demographic appeals through the image of technology itself. Notably, construction on the park began in 1975, a year after Disney World's attendance dropped more than 17% (Fjellmen 1992, 134). Moreover, many of EPCOT's corporate stories spun in imagery, display, and devices like Worldkey and IEDs that bespoke a more intimate, responsive, and individualized relationship for users of technology.[3] In a presciently critical assessment of the park drafted near its initial opening, Gersh Morningstar (1983) attacked this individualization as an invasion, stating:

> Ma Bell is going to walk abroad the land, ready to insinuate her way into every household, having the capability to turn the home TV set into an interactive information, communication, and entertainment center . . . and while this is going on someone in a Mickey Mouse suit is going to be coming around convincing everyone that they want this capability and teaching them how to use it (29).

Or, more formally, the park's exhibits became part of the wholesale political-economic effort to craft an interactive subject position for users. By 1994, most of the videodisc-powered innovations of the original EPCOT had been removed, along with several of the park's original corporate sponsors, but the topoi of interactivity and its articulated connection to neoliberal corporate agility and deterritorialized individuality remain.

For the remainder of this chapter, I will further discuss the sociotechnical context of *Dragon's Lair* by constructing a more exhaustive archeology of early interactivity, putting the game into conversation with several contemporary videodisc and interactive TV inventions, some made and many more simply proposed. This deep context will situate *Dragon's Lair* as one attempt among many to reconfigure media business and users by examining the U.S. patent records of so-called interactive TV systems and by more specifically outlining production histories for other notable applications of the videodisc: Robert Abel's *CubeQuest* (1983) and Lucasfilm and Convergence's *Editdroid* (1983). A preponderance of contemporary examples will reveal the discourse that constituted a historically prior understanding of interactivity, its uses, its functions, and ultimately its ideology. But first, I will attempt to address modern criticisms and understandings of *Dragon's Lair* as a design failure by historicizing the very notion of interactivity. It is my hope that this chapter will free *Dragon's Lair* from the analytic fate as a bad design object or as a stepping stone in larger technological evolution of videogames and, instead, cast it as a provocative symptom of a larger attempt to reinterpret and redefine our relationship to filmed media in the moment of neoliberalism.

THE AESTHETICS OF INTERACTIVITY, OR WHY *DRAGON'S LAIR* "SUCKED"

Traditionally, evaluative critics of *Dragon's Lair* have ranked the game very low. By evaluative critics, I am referring to analysts who use the notion of interactivity as a mark, measure, or threshold to be obtained in games and other systems. In the estimation of these critics, to not reach this threshold evinces a failure of design or at least an inadequate gaming experience. These analysts frequently cite *Dragon's Lair* as a game that fails to measure up to these standards. Demonstrative of this attitude is designer Greg Costikyan's emphatic appraisal:

> As a game, however, [*Dragon's Lair*] sucked. Essentially, you watched an animation clip lasting a few seconds, and had to quickly make a choice by moving the joystick in one direction or another. One choice led to death. The other triggered another few seconds of animation and another choice. You played by feeding in quarter after quarter and learning which choices didn't make you die through a process of rote memorization. Not surprisingly, the sequels failed.

For Costikyan, financial failure was overdetermined by a simplistic design and an underwhelming and possibly exploitative experience, neither of which passed the threshold of adequate interactivity in the writer's estimation. The sentiment and premise can be tracked in contemporary commentary on *Dragon's Lair* and its many ports to other gaming platforms that while noting, sometimes begrudgingly, the perceived importance of the game, mark its overall failure of interactivity, or its other critical euphemisms (playability, controls, etc.):

- "The gameplay is as simple (and boring) as it gets" (Smith 2006);
- "Of course, by today's standards, the gameplay is simplistic and unforgiving" (Arn 2009);
- "it can be said that the person who benefits the most from a *Dragon's Lair* experience is the person watching the game being played" (Moriarty 2012);
- "This collection [*Dragon's Lair* and its sequels] should be viewed more as an interactive museum piece, rather than on the merits of its gameplay" (Sweeting 2019).

This brief sample of retrospective analyses suggests how central interactivity is to the assessment of videogames and, frankly, how *Dragon's Lair* is viewed as a bad object when it is used as an evaluative metric. Yet the exact process of measuring interactivity is left mostly implied or assumed in these reviews.

In a more value-neutral manner, many academic critics of videogames and new media have attempted to outline a clearer aesthetics of interactivity, proposing theoretical definitions and taxonomies of its application in practice to guide both the construction and criticism of system design and user experience. And while these critics avoid the judgmental posture of their evaluative counterparts, many of their theoretical projects similarly mark *Dragon's Lair* as a problematic outlier and perhaps not even "interactive" at all. Drawing on poststructuralist's theory's celebration of deferred meaning textual porousness, Marie-Laure Ryan's (1994) early and influential examination of interactivity defined the concept as "dynamic simulation." Specifically, interactivity is used to describe a new class of aesthetic experiences concerned not with linear plotting but in spatial exploration, not with stable reference worlds but with constant reconfiguration, and not with reliance on signs to communicate meaning but with what Ryan calls the materiality of the medium, presumably the thing-like existence of virtual flora and fauna felt as independent of outward mediation. Expanding on their own work as game designers, Michael Mataes and Andrew Stern (2004) elaborated upon Ryan's initial work, but used the metaphors of theater and dialogue instead of literature and navigation. For these authors, interactivity was only experienced not simply when a system responds to a user but when there is a balance between what they call a system's material and formal causes or between what a user can and should do. And in a brief but authoritative piece, Mark J. P. Wolf (2006) refocused the role of interactivity from system response to user choice. In this piece, Wolf usefully charted a list of design parameters in the organization of player decisions such as breadth, that is how many choices a user is exposed to, speed, that is at what rate users are exposed to choices and how quickly they must respond, and communicativeness, that is how perfect is a user's knowledge of choices and their possible consequences. Despite the differing focuses, all these authors shared a similar intention of generating a common language to describe and analyze a form of textual experience without an established critical lexicon.

As exemplary as these classificatory systems are in their construction, they provide little room for a seemingly idiosyncratic work like *Dragon's Lair*. The game certainly approaches the lush virtual worlds that Ryan underlines in her definition, yet because of the pre-recorded material, the game fails to present a fluid environment indicative of her notion of interactivity. Similarly, the evocative imagery of the game likely over-inflates user desire for action— Why can't I use my sword now? Why can't I jump now? and so on—generating an unbalance and dissonance of what Mataes and Stern call material and formal cause. And lastly, if interrogated using Wolf's parameters, *Dragon's Lair* is a game of limited aesthetic application: in terms of breadth, users are not given many choices; in terms of speed, users are only intermittently given choices and in punishingly short windows of response; and in terms of communicativeness, user's availability of choice and their relative chance for success is often only really apparent in multiple playthroughs. In other words, although *Dragon's Lair* might not be inadequately interactive as interpreted by evaluative critics, it is, in the emerging standards of aesthetic critics, a severely limited execution of the evolving concept.

Dragon's Lair was created by a particular configuration of temporal ordering and spatial representation that constitutes an organization of response, agency, and choice atypical of works that would be held up by evaluative or aesthetic minded critics as successful or interesting examples of so-called interactivity. The game presents a world highly rich in detail, indeed rooms such as the wizard's laboratory (see fig. 3.2) and the bedroom trap are littered with objects to misdirect and attract a user's attention; however, the game denies the user the temporal latitude, that is, the "time," to investigate these details. This places *Dragon's Lair* in direct opposition to later adventure-themed games in which the experience was dominated by user's scanning for and clicking on—or interacting with—with represented objects, as in the popular games of Rand and Robyn Miller such as *The Manhole* (1983) and *Myst* (1993).

Figure 3.2 The Cluttered Wizard's Laboratory in _Dragon's Lair_ (2017). _Source_: Screenshot captured from the Digital Leisure PS4 port.

Figure 3.3 The Many Unusable Doors in the Haunted Crypt in _Dragon's Lair_ (2017). _Source_: Screenshot captured from the Digital Leisure PS4 port.

Also, _Dragon's Lair_ displays to its users a setting dense in spatial possibilities indicated in many untaken and inaccessible portals depicted in such rooms as the haunted crypt (see fig. 3.3), the earthquake trap, and the underground rapids. The game marks many of these passages as arbitrarily "wrong" choices, while many others are not attached to a possible choice at all, but the larger point is that the game restricts a user's spatial latitude to either investigate setting or even change perspective. Subsequent games that incorporated pre-recorded elements, like so-called interactive movies (see Perron et al. 2008) such as Roberta Williams's *Phantasmagoria* (1995) and multi-media CD-roms such as Vince Lee's[4] *Rebel Assault* (1993) amended explorability by providing multiple perspectives on setting, in the former case, and by superimposing sprite graphics onto pre-recorded elements, in the latter case. To put it more simply, *Dragon's Lair* combined the visual design of an adventure game with the mechanics of an action game. And while this hybridization ultimately resulted in a game being retrospectively dissonant with notions of interactivity, it was a heady mix clearly overdetermined by technical capabilities of the time as well as the economic mandate and game design brief discussed in previous chapters. Coin drop was dependent not on user absorption but quick failure and user "death." And the game operated mostly as a series of optical tricks which challenged users precisely to not be absorbed into the ornate elaboration of the depicted space. While these choices may not comport with modern conceptions of interactivity, they recur throughout the patent records of other proposed uses of videodiscs and interactive TV systems.

THE "PAPER WORLD" OF EARLY SCREEN INTERACTIVITY

Although decoding historical documents like patents is challenging from the perspective of media studies, the exercise can reveal minute detail and abstractions, ideal for critical interpretation. As legal documents, patent records must itemize and explain the unique functions and capabilities of their proposed devices to attain the threshold of idea property. At this level, the documents offer an image of a device as executable and are likely only interesting to technicians concerned with their feasibility and possible alternative applications. However, patents typically are not just technical notes. Because inventors, and their named employers, use these documents to expand their possible ownership over derivative devices, patents often include speculation on future uses, usually referred to as "preferred embodiments." And because inventors must demonstrate their device's unique features, patents conventionally describe current problems or dilemmas in their technical subfields, often dubbed "prior art limitations," in order to articulate their proposal's newness. And lastly, patents often partake in what can be termed self-promotion, celebrating the social or cultural desires that their device intends to satisfy. In other words, patent documents are not simply objective descriptions of the electro-chemico-mechanical operation of technical devices; they are equally textual constructions deeply involved in discursive articulation and future speculation.

As mentioned, *Dragon's Lair* was just one of many inventions seeking to use videodiscs to create interactive TV experiences. While a handful of these inventions were operationalized, and even fewer were commercialized, most exist primarily in the "paper world" (Hughes 2016, 46) of patents. However, their relative material absence as tangible devices only speaks to the conditions and interest in these new screen inventions or as historian Johnathan Coopersmith (2009) aptly put it, "failure often indicates the perception of opportunity" (95). In addition to evincing the larger themes of social crisis and causation sketched in this chapter's final section, these patents also outline a set of desires and expectations around the emerging construction of interactivity, once again at odds with contemporary evaluative and aesthetic definitions. In this experimental moment for the concept, interactivity was frequently framed more as a measure of user control and a measure of uniqueness of experience. A vision for this holistically new screen interaction was most eloquently described in documents filed by Preston Blair and Frank Preston's (1987) "TV animation interactively controlled by the viewer" and Robert Best's (1981) "Dialog between TV movies and human viewers."

Although its makers never realized it into a marketable device, the Blair and Preston invention, in its patent description, raises many of the hopes for TV's interactive future. Blair, like Don Bluth, was a traditional cel animator by trade, working in the cartoon studios for Disney, MGM and Hanna-Barbera, but he is probably best remembered as an author of drawing and animation instructional books such as *Cartoon Animation*, which has been in nearly continuous print since 1980. In their invention, Blair and Preston proposed using animated key frames, moments of extreme character movement artistically bridged by work of in-between artists in the industrial process of animation, as user decision points and mechanical switching points in a multitrack video player. The system was to use these drawings, imperceptible in viewing but key in the hierarchy of cartoon labor, as hinge points in variability, allowing for "rapid and repeated switching from and to continuously radically different types of action smoothly, logically, and according to dramatics" (1). Later the authors describe their invention as a

> system of multiple scenes interactively switched by the action of the user and multiple episodes that may be determined by random choice, user action, or user choice [that] creates such a complexity of graphic pattern and dramatic odds that the uncertainties of life are simulated although animation is pre-photographed, pre-recorded, and pre-programmed (3).

In the patent, the old media techniques of animation cycles are recombined to offer a sense of user agency and individual uniqueness of experience, constituting a qualitatively new experience of media. The patent concludes rhapsodically charting the textual possibilities for the system:

> Suspense and dramatic situations place the player in simulated danger on in positions requiring skills and reflex action. Such animation simulates, for example, the three dimensional visual action confronting the eye of a space traveler, an explorer attacked by ancient monsters in an unknown land resembling the pre-historic, an underwater swimmer attacked by huge sharks, octopuses, torpedos from enemy submarines, and frogmen denizens of the deep. An eskimo is attached [*sic*] by polar bears and wolves. On an African Safari rhinos, elephants and attack the player. Based on World War I airplanes, an aerial dogfight casts the player in the cockpit of a plane being attached [*sic*] by on-coming planes and destroying enemy planes and dirigibles according the accuracy of his gun. (13)

An uncommonly passionate section for a patent, this section breathlessly cycles through a series of popular culture narratives of masculine adventure, simultaneously projecting and inhibiting the use of the device within the cultural frame of these scenarios. In the same passage the authors continue to draw on the appeal of popular culture and genre storytelling stating: "Superman, Batman, Bugs Bunny, The Hulk, Wonder Woman, friendly space creatures and the likes of Dick Tracy help, talk to the player questions about strategy, and act accordingly to the player's verbal response as described in the previously references Best patent" (13).

The Best referred to in this quotation was Robert Best who had already proposed his own interactive TV system that combined pre-recorded material with user choice and multiple sequencing. Or, in the words of the inventor, "the apparatus can . . . provide each viewer with the illusion of individualized and active participation" (1). Best was an independent computer researcher who often focused on issues of encryption and natural language processing and so, unsurprisingly, his invention was to be controlled by a human operator's voice. Natural conversation as a standard for human-computer interface has a long history beginning with Alan Turing's imitation game and continues on into contemporary philosophical discussions of interaction (see, e.g., Smuts 2009) and in commercial vaporware (as described in chapter 2). Best's proposal likely, too, became a direct or indirect influence on Rick Dyer's own attempt to integrate natural language into his Halcyon device. And although Best's exact machine was never realized on a large scale, it arguably resonated with a broader interest and desire for different screen experiences, receiving coverage in the *New York Times* and several other popular periodicals. A short, hyperbolic piece in the forward-looking *OMNI* quoted the inventor who claimed, "twenty years from now when interactive movies are commonplace . . . today's movies will seem as crude as silent movies" (Hoban 1982, 21).

Despite the grandness of their claims, which must in part be understood as acts of self-promotion, both Best as well as Blair and Preston spell out the definitive limitations of their conception of interactivity, providing a series of workarounds and design choices that both echo and prefigure the construction of *Dragon's Lair*. In the first case, the inventors situate their respective machines in embodiments saturated with what we can call genre material or popular culture frames of reference which both guide and limit player action. The long quote from Blair and Preston above and other accompanying passages spell out violent, fight-or-flight scenarios, everything from dragon attacks, to western shootouts, to underwater shark attacks. In this patent document, the inventors also included a detailed step diagram, listed as "Figure 21," in order to minutely demonstrate the operation of the device (see fig. 3.4). And as an

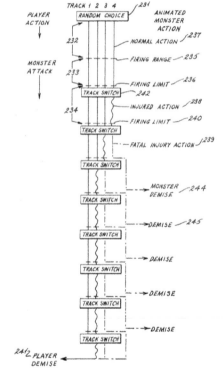

Figure 3.4   Detail from "TV Animation Interactively Controlled by the Viewer" by Preston Blair and Frank Preston (1987). *Source: United States Patent 4,711,543; Filed on Dec. 8, 1987. Retrieved from Google Patents Database.*

example, the inventors supplied the diagram with the hypothetical content of an "animated monster attack." Similarly, Best's examples, too, draw on scenarios of quick-paced, fantasy combat. The top page of the patent record even includes a crude drawing of a user choosing to run from a group of club-armed trolls amassing in the game's monitor and leering toward the player (see fig. 3.5). These colorful descriptions respond to already set conventions and presumed use preference for simulated violence in early videogame design.[5] The choice, too, was likely informed by the elegance and Boolean simplicity of violent interactions (fight-run, win-lose) and, therefore, their ease of description in technical protocols. And, this proposed choice of outward material also speaks to what these inventors understood as the limitations and possibilities of their hypothetical hardware. Besides indicating the specific preferred genres of game design, these inventors suggested that their systems were only really suitable for brief interactions, which would allow for the devices to limit choice and manage response. As Best states, "because of practical limitation, the apparatus is most suited to melodramatic serials or series with short, self-contained episodes" (11). Brevity is stressed in both Blair and Preston's descriptions. For example, the inventors describe the use of their device to emulate a game of tennis (or perhaps pong), a game that can be boiled down to intermittent bursts of user action, limited responses to action (hit or miss), and frequent

Figure 3.5   Detail from "Dialog between TV Movies and Human Viewers" by Robert Best (1981). *Source: United States Patent 4,305,131; Filed on Dec. 8, 1981. Retrieved from Google Patents.*

pauses between volleys and games. Further, Best listed even more design tricks of what he called "disguised repetition" (11) that could be employed by forcing branching players into repeated "neutral" scenes, or re-usable scenes, and that game footage could be re-used also by replacing the accompanying audio track during subsequent replays, thereby giving new descriptions to repeated imagery. Constructed with the same limitations and possibilities, and a consequently similar notion of interactivity, *Dragon's Lair*, as discussed throughout, gravitated toward many of these same workarounds, relying on genre imagery and narrative device (discussed at length in Chapter Four) to motivate and limit players, segmenting the play into brief portions (in Dyer's terminology, "rooms"), disguising repetition with repeated neutral scenes (for example, the repeated skeletal loop played after each "death"), and the re-using of optically inverted rooms. By reading these patent records and placing *Dragon's Lair* in conversation, we can then reconstruct a virtual debate and emerging consensus between inventors, via their respective patents and inventions, on the emerging standards of interactivity.

Also, part of this debate was a consideration around how precisely users were to manipulate pre-photographed material. In other words, the frustration of denying the ability to navigate or give a sense of constant, virtual presence was very much on the minds of inventors of the time. As a novel solution, Best's device was built around voice recognition. And while Blair and Preston's preferred embodiment was to employ the tracking of user movement in physical space with "ultrasonic position detector," the inventors also hedged their bets suggesting that the apparatus could work with a "mouse, a tracking ball, and a joystick" (9). Several other contemporary videodisc and interactive TV patents alternatively suggested that video and game elements could be combined by keeping each separate. A patent filed by researchers working for videodisc maker Philips (Kroon and Robers 1984) proposed a system of multiple interconnected monitors, one for the display of audio-visual material and the other to display separately encoded disc information. In essence, the patent describes a style of digital information panels that would become standard for most home electronics, and also recalls *Dragon's Lair* own solution to maintain game information (score and lives) on a separate "monitor" with its own dedicated RAM. And previously, Ralph Baer (1982), along with his collaborator Leonard Cope, secured a patent for an "Interactive playback system" that proposed to situate stored pre-recorded visual material on a layer "beneath" a layer of machine and user-controlled game elements. The patent describes a seemingly unmade videodisc version of pinball in which the table's bumpers and flippers were photographed, stored and reproduced from media stored on the disc. Also, to be included in the disc tracks were data dumps describing the discrete screen location of these represented obstacles. An attached computer would have controlled and generated the game's moveable elements such as the ball and the score display. The proposed apparatus lastly was designed to manage dynamic relationship between pre-recorded and computer-generated elements, between the user-engaged microprocessor and the TV signal, via the mechanism of simple collision, that is the ball "hitting" the bumpers. This core idea of superimposing videodisc-based media and microprocessor-based games was attempted by several firms—Atari's *Firefox* (1983) and Sega's *Astron Belt* (1983)—during the initial "laser craze." But, more broadly, the concept informs the management of assets in modern videogames engineering.

Additionally, all these earlier videodisc and interactive TV patents struggled with the mechanical question of how to accommodate the switching or branching of content in quick response to user input. The very premise that a user could switch was conceptually dependent on the notion that a single TV signal could include either additional information or could be understood as "deep." Surprisingly, many of the important innovations pointing toward this understanding of TV predated the invention of videodiscs and or popularization of videogames. By 1959, researchers at RCA had earned a patent demonstrating the feasibility of including facsimile messages within regular TV broadcasts (Beers 1959), a process refined later with composite TV signals (Houghton 1970). Moreover, several researchers pursued the idea for multiplexing not only text information (which would become the basis of closed captioning), but also completely alternative broadcasts. In 1968, Marvin Camras, an engineer partially responsible for the invention of multi-track audio recording on magnetic tape, earned a patent for a similar process in which physical fields of videotape could be apportioned to parallel information tracks. Five years later, a scientist working for Westinghouse registered a patent demonstrating how multiple picture signals could be shared on a single over-the-air broadcast by using signal filters to allow for what the inventor called "line sharing" (Justice 1973). A more elegant solution was offered in another Ralph Baer patent for a "Dual image television" (1976), which used the interlaced even and odd fields of the NTSC TV broadcast to send and receive two distinct, multiplexed programs.[6] This quick review of patent history demonstrates that the notion that the TV signal could contain additional information or variable content that a user could switch between predated videodisc, but significantly it was only pursued when interactivity became a new industrial and, arguably, social imperative (as discussed in the final section of the chapter). Regardless of the causation, later inventors gravitated to the videodisc for its ability to now facilitate multiplicity through its unique capabilities of frame address and random access. But even these systems were inhibited by the historical limitations of RAM as well as the raw speed of the physical movement of the laser stylus across the disc surface. Dale Rodesch, an inventor mostly associated with video poker, slot machines, and gambling machines (see Harpster 2010), earned a patent for his "Interactive video disc system" (1984) which proposed a unique solution. This machine worked using a disc player with three reading heads, two fixed and one mobile, allowing for, what the inventor called, "true interaction" (1). In the preferred embodiment of the patent—a simple outer space shooter game—the fixed heads remain always ready to read and display turn-concluding explosions. Meanwhile a scientist at RCA fielded a patent also addressing this mechanical problem, proposing a dual-head videodisc player in which one head always playing while the other one was always scanning and cuing (Altman 1983). Both were novel solutions, but largely unavailable to *Dragon's Lair* and other videogames built with commercially available videodisc players. Regardless, these patents collectively demonstrate that *Dragon's Lair*'s conception of multiplicity in TV signals as well as the limit challenge of buffering, belongs not just the history of videogame, but also to the longer lineage of interactive TV.

In his short piece on technology and historiography, Carrol Pursell (2001) argued that the work of the historian lies less in charting how technological devices work, or worked and more in how they "mean." Indeed, as a media studies scholar, I have a limited capacity to unpack precisely how all the above-mentioned inventions were designed to work or even if any was really a good idea in the broadest of terms. However, I do contend that they collectively can be read as a cross section of inventors thinking about their respective devices and the underlying, unsettled concept of interactivity. All these inventors imagined a qualitatively different relationship between users and screen media, but this new engagement could only be achieved by the construction of specific design applications, the minimization or reduction of user activity, and the management of the physics of discs themselves, all problems equally investigated in the design and hardware of *Dragon's Lair*. In the final section of this chapter, I will continue to unpack the meaning of the rush toward videodisc and interactive TV systems and pose it as a deeper symptom of neoliberalism's idealization of the active or interactive subject. But first, I will use two extended examples of two other videodisc "failures" to consider how interactivity was framed also as an industrial mandate and an entrepreneurial opportunity in an uncertain business.

INTERACTIVITY AS STRATEGY:
CUBEQUEST AND EDITDROID

Given the game's initial success, it might be odd to consider *Dragon's Lair* a failure. However, several facts owing to the long life of the text have contributed to that popular assignation. By the makers' own estimates, sales of the cabinet were much below expectations. The partnership of the original creators quickly dissolved in the aftermath, scrapping plans for a subsequent videodisc games line. Further, *Dragon's Lair* and its fellow videodisc games did not save the business of arcades as was, perhaps unrealistically, hoped, and that business continued to face declines. In the years since the game's release, *Dragon's Lair*'s design has served as a perpetual historical footnote and often negative example, giving life to historian Kenneth Lipartito's (2003) observation that "socially constructed failures are also socially reso-nant, and they shape our options for the future" (57). In other words, even if *Dragon's Lair* is deemed by cultural and industrial authorities a failure, its significance in the contested space of the social imagination around technol-ogy and media is difficult to discount.

In this section, I will follow Lipartito's (2003) contention and suggest how so-called failures, like *Dragon's Lair*, along with the many realized and unre-alized videodisc and interactive TV applications of the time, provide insight into the contingency and struggle over an "open-ended technological world" (57). More specifically, I will use two comparative case studies of two other contemporary uses of the videodisc—Robert Abel's work on *CubeQuest* and Lucasfilm and Covergence's Editdroid—to help bring *Dragon's Lair* into better relief. In the press coverage, the videodisc was referred to as an every-thing disk owing to its technical ability to encode many forms of information. But, as demonstrated in the following histories, the "everything" could just as well symbolize the medium's projected potential in the estimation of media makers who leveraged its potential to cross verticals and practice speculative entrepreneurialism.

This section also draws on the example of several recent media historians examining other productive instances of failure in media technology. In his work on Nintendo's Virtual Boy format, Steven Boyer (2009) argues that that invention's weak performance on the marketplace indicates the interplay, and ultimate dissonance between marketing promises and consumer desires around changing expectations of interactivity, a struggle already resonant with the jagged response to *Dragon's Lair*. Jacob Mertens's (2021) investi-gation of the controversy and dissatisfaction around the release of the more recent videogame *Assassin's Creed Unity* (2014) argues that this game's per-ceived failure illustrates the contested negotiation around a new digital ser-vices business model for games publishing as it is integrated by both makers and users. And, in Kit Hughes's (2016) deep historical examination of CBS's proto homevideo EVR system, the author demonstrates how what she calls "threshold media" provide institutions and inventors an opportunity to dis-cursively rehearse the newness and promise of new media. In all these stud-ies, the so-called failure of these inventions serves to illustrate precisely the uncertainty and struggle on the part of makers and users, as well as their real and textual relationships with one another that both Lipartito and Huhtamo would call the very stuff of media history. The below capsule histories of "failure" will then help bring more of the redundant themes and debates at the core of *Dragon's Lair*, as both a designed machine and more specifically as a business strategy, more clear.

The career of designer Robert Abel, who used an eager embrace of first traditional visual effects and eventual computer imagery to great critical acclaim and financial success in the late 1970s and early 1980s, offers one such productive example. Trading on deep pedigree that included time with John Whitney Sr., Saul Bass, and Charles Eames, Abel founded a production house, which rose to prominence thanks mostly to their integration of visual effects. Their "Bubbles" (1974) commercial for 7-Up used compositing and backlit animation to execute an effective collage of popular culture imagery contained in a single, continuously forward camera "movement." The striking ad embodied the Abel ethic of using commercials as "30 second test-sites for innovative technique" ("Abel to Host . . ." 1984, 55). Subsequent to this initial success, Abel & Associates increased its effects work, famously purchasing an Evans & Sutherland Picture System II. The firm modified the E&S machine, originally intended for aircraft design and aerospace research, to produce meticulous pre-visualizations for their commercial work (important for pitching client), to program motion-controlled cameras for effects work, and to generate then state-of-the art line vector graphic images and animations straight from the computer terminal. The studio used wire-frame imagery as a recurring housestyle, appearing in advertising work, like Panasonic's "Glider" (1981) ad and their work on building the images of the virtual environments, or "game grid," in the feature film *TRON*. These and similarly designed works contributed greatly to the clean, neon look that defined the visual culture of the era and style still recognized as stereotypically "80s." Through its embrace of new technology, Abel's firm secured cross over work across film, TV, an advertising boasting, in addition to the E&S system, six motion-controlled camera and two optical printers. In other words, Abel's house had the capability to produce any type of filmed imagery whole cloth. The firm also expanded its business into other revenue streams. As early as 1981, Abel and Associates promoted the sale of its own purpose-built hardware-software suites; by 1984 it formed its own filmed entertainment division, principally to produce music videos, then an emerging new genre; and by 1985, it formed Abel Image Research, a division devoted solely to digital image production ("What's New . . ." 1981; Goldman 1984a; "Abel Launches . . ." 1985). Notably, the firm's house ads from the time bragged, "and you thought that we were just an effects company."

Rapid expansion and devotion to new technology at Abel likely was in response to business initiative and market demand, and should also be understood in the context of the advertising industry's own perceived institutional crisis. In the wake of the greater appreciation for the active or interactive consumer as well as the increasing density of increasingly individualized mediascape often called information overload, or more pejoratively, clutter, the ad business bemoaned a perceived loss of viewer attention. Abel's strategy in response was twofold: expand the firm's capabilities and overdrive the imagery, both aims advanced by and through an embrace of new media technologies. Abel himself frankly diagnosed the context in a contemporary article on the "feature film look" in advertising stating, "the situation has grown out of a heightened awareness of visual product . . . [commercials] can't just look like the same crap one sees on TV" (Cardona 1985, 12). The sentiment was also conveyed by Abel collaborator Bill Kovacs's (1980) earlier assessment that "the old and much copied FX, such as simple streaking and slit scan, no longer provide the visual impact they once did" (78).[7]

Among the many specific media technologies that Abel and his firm touted in their ample press coverage of the time was the videodisc and its potential for so-called interactivity. During the 1970s, Abel also worked as a producer of rock concert films like *Mad Dogs and Englishmen* (1971) and *Let the Good Times Roll* (1973). The designer leveraged this experience in his pitch for a new "song-interactive entertainment," which proposed to use the videodisc to salvage the recording industry then experiencing a post-Disco, pre-MTV slump. Simply, the idea was to capture live concerts in such a way that a "user can manipulate the image" in is replay (McCullaugh 1980, VM-1). At a video music conference, Abel explained more elaborately stating, "when I did rock films, we used 12 or more cameras, and most of the material wound up being thrown away . . . the video disk is a digital medium where you can mix, match, and interact," simultaneously ceding choice and avoiding waste (Forrest 1981). Although Abel produced an effects-laden proto-music video, promotional film for the Jacksons's album *Triumph* (1980), most of the designer's ideas for "song-interactive entertainment" were unrealized but added the immense discourse around videodiscs and their textual and industrial potential. However, Abel did apply some of these same ideals into his lone venture into videogame production, *CubeQuest*.

The videogame industry, a media business defined by its relationship to new technology and striking graphics, was another likely field for expansion for Abel's plan to seek out visually savvy consumers, and in October 1983, he contributed to the videodisc game entitled *CubeQuest*. The tile was produced by Simultrek, a partnership with Abel and Kovacs, the later of whom had previously described the venture stating, "we're making preparations for the next generation of videogames . . . [and] we want to bring a director's point of view into videogames [in which] the visuals are going to become much more important" (Levinsohn 1982, 62). Clearly, in the boom before the bust in for videogames, the medium was very much on the minds of Abel and his collaborators. In 1982, the production house produced a two-minute theatrical commercial for Atari to play on international screens and also created a 7-Up campaign, entitled "Play to Win," starring the then ubiquitous Pac-Man consuming the soft drink's trademarked red dots ("Abel's Effects . . ." 1982; "Abel Plays . . ." 1982).[8]

Like *Dragon's Lair*, *CubeQuest* was a hybrid platform, integrating gaming components with a videodisc player. However, unlike *Dragon's Lair*, *CubeQuest* combined these components, following the suggestion of Baer's "Interactive playback system," by superimposing two separate layers: in the foreground was a vector game mechanically independent of a background layer which displayed series of animation loops stored and reproduced from a videodisc. The top layer, the playable portion of the game containing its avatar, its MOBs, and its scoring, is a z-axis shooter like *Tempest* (1981) or *Gyruss* (1983) in which a player "moves" infinitely toward the screen center. This portion of the game was produced mostly by designer Paul Allen Newell using Parker Brothers's Vectrex game engine before Newell and his collaborators ported it to a system of their own design (Stilphen 2008). Abel and his collaborators were then responsible for the background imagery which mimicked the same inward motion with a series of recursive loops, some graphically abstract and others illogically incorporating representations of corridors, caverns, or jungle foliage. The continuous, uncut, z-axis movement has a long aesthetic history effects work, going back at least as far as the "Jupiter and Beyond" section in *2001: A Space Odyssey* (1968), becoming the textual basis for what Vivian Sobchack (1997) called the virtual subject position of electronic media. The virtual camera movement was also another element of industrial house style for Abel's studio, traceable through much of their work across media, in everything from the slow push in the signature "Bubbles" ad, to Flynn's entry into the computerized world of *TRON*, to the opening, swooping time travel titles produced for Steven Spielberg's television series *Amazing Stories* (1985–1987). The Abel footage for *CubeQuest* also contains many signature Abel effects—light streaking and slitscan sequences—and recycled imagery—neon vector lines and glowing bubbles. The loops and their repeating patterns also give the impression of op art or tessellation, visual techniques also popular at Abel & Associates thanks to their award-winning "Changing Pictures" ad for TRW (1983) which was loosely based on M.C. Escher's woodcut "Sky and Water I" (1938).[9]

Although *CubeQuest* was Abel's and Simultrek's only attempt at videogame production—the cabinet was released in October 1983 and the firm shuttered the following January—their single game indicates much about the contemporary debates around interactivity as both a creative endeavor and a business practice. Like *Dragon's Lair, CubeQuest*, by modern standards suffers from too evocative of imagery, suggesting a multitude of lines of attention, interest, and desire, none of which could accommodate engagement. Game footage from *CubeQuest*'s interlocking layers depicts a visual density that is often hard to decipher, making this imagery part of the challenge of the game's design. The game then is better understood as a visual experiment precisely about the notion of information overload that Abel frequently discussed and a user's ability to deal with this bombardment. In other words, both *Dragon's Lair* and *CubeQuest* are games of visual intelligence, presenting players with a set of filmic puzzles and taxing players' focus and attention. Moreover, the business rationale behind each demonstrates a similar strategy, using a nascent, unformed medium, the videodisc itself, to navigate an industrial moment of uncertainty and entrepreneurial possibility. In the case of the later, Abel had a significant model. During press coverage, Abel often cited the example of George Lucas, and his Lucasfilm and ILM divisions, as the standard of a "modern studio . . . [where] synergy among different filmmaking disciplines is nurtured" ("Abel to Host . . ." 1984, 55). Unsurprisingly, Lucasfilm was yet another contemporary firm where much promise and potential was anticipated in the videodisc.

After five years of development, Lucasfilm introduced its non-linear film editing suite, Editdroid, to much curiosity and speculation at the 1984 National Association of Broadcasters conference.[10] The device, which used commercially available Sony and Panasonic videodisc players to facilitate film editing, was part of the firm's plan to expand their specialties through the adoption of new media technology. Most famously Lucasfilm had diversified with the formation of the visual effects house Industrial Light and Magic, the computer image and animation studio Pixar, as well as less well-known attempts to move into the business of media technology components themselves. In 1983, the firm began to promote its own Cadroid, a hardware-software suite for design work ("Lucasfilm Unveils . . ." 1983). And in the same year, the film trades reported on Lucasfilm's planned "interactive TV system" that was to be built in collaboration with Nolan Bushnell's Silicon Valley incubator, Catalyst, yet never materialized ("New Black Box . . ." 1983). Like *Dragon's Lair* and *CubeQuest*, the Editdroid was a joint venture, in this case between Lucas and Convergence, a Southern Californian computer firm. Although the marketing of the Editdroid posed it as science fiction innovation—notably naming its physical components "planets" and "suns"—recurrent pitches in the contemporary press framed the suite as one that would restore both efficiency and individual direction on the work of film editing. Pointedly, the initial slogan for the device was the wordy: "not just triumph in technology but a triumph in editing craftsmanship." The ballyhoo around Editdroid promised less distractions in the work of editing specifically by eliminating the need to log choices in arbitrary time codes, to re-record masters and cuts with each new revision, to manually shuttle through footage, and to physically set film reels, all resulting in a workflow that was promoted as being at least twice as fast as traditional flatbed film editing (Solomon 1984). This boasted simplification reportedly included Lucas's own specifications for the device to have an absolute minimum of buttons and limited user interaction with numbers in order to refocus attention on the relations of images and sequences ("Editdroid, Lucasfilm . . ." 1984). Moreover, the system was promoted as one designed for an editor to work individually from "one's own lap" without the need for facilitating assistants (Goldman 1984b, 40). Notably, all the advertising imagery depicts the suite accompanied by a lone plush office chair—one "player" at a time.

The Editdroid was not the only non-linear editing system introduced at the 1984 NAB; in fact, the device was announced at a significant moment in the overall computerization of film and media creative work. Press coverage from *Broadcasting* described this transition best stating,

> the most common type of equipment at the National Association of Broadcasters exhibition . . . was not cameras or videotape recorders or monitors or transmitters or any type of hardware traditionally associated with a broadcast station or a production studio. The most common type of equipment was the computer. ("NAB '84 . . ." 1984, 46)

The Editdroid itself was introduced alongside high profile launches for Montage and CMX's own digital editing systems, reflecting the overriding fervor for computerization itself across domains of work and leisure sketched in chapter 2. Although the Editdroid was not alone in the emerging market for non-linear editing systems, it was the only device engineered specifically to take advantage of the unique features of the videodisc, features that played an equally prominent role in the videogame design. One writer for *Billboard* made this connection explicit reporting,

> the computer-controlled videodisk, the fickle darling of the arcade game industry, is becoming the basis of a new breed of electronic pictures editing systems for creative visual producers in which technology is made "so transparent you can practically hold the image in your hand." (Winslow 1984, 30)

Specifically, the Editdroid's operation relied on the videodisc's capabilities for individual frame address and non-linear access of footage. In the years before Editdroid and other non-linear systems, editors often worked by logging footage with video time code; however, accessing specifically coded film material still necessitated mechanical shuttling. And in order to view provisional "cuts" of footage, editors needed to create provisional re-recorded masters. By combining the Editdroid with several videodisc players, editors could create a live preview of several minutes without any manual shuttling or re-recording (Goldman 1984b, 39). Instant access and "real time" previews essentially are givens in today's editing workflows, but were significant advancements in their own time for their integration of work and creative practice. But I am more interested in how these core innovations mark the Editdroid as a companion device to *Dragon's Lair*. Both rely heavily on the frame address to facilitate quick recall through traditionally filmed, and digitally encoded footage, and both use the videodisc to construct virtual film narratives, one in the form of a playthrough and the other in the form of a virtual cut. More simply, both can be understood as an early attempt to reshape film as a so-called interactive medium.

Despite the lack of adoption, the backstory of Editdroid's own "failure" displays many of the themes in the creation of the interactive subject and the industrial strategy projected on the invention of the videodisc, making it historically productive if not technically so. According to Deron Overpeck (2016), Lucasfilm only ever managed to sell 20 Editdroids, owing to either their technical unreliability or an overly expensive price. Ironically, both non-linear editing and disk-based media became central to both the creative practice and the business of the media industries in the following decade. The design choices and the motivations supporting the construction of the Editdroid, however, suggest more historical attempts to define and frame interactivity itself. In the first case, the Editdroid promised to simplify and re-individualize the creative practice of editing itself, an impulse resonate with larger political-economic themes of neoliberalism and their influence on technical inventions, as discussed in the following section. This interpretive frame for the device also resonates with Julie Turnock's (2015) contention that 1970s Hollywood auteurs, like Lucas, experimented with visual effects and new technology, at first, to support generating a more authentic, singular vision in their filmmaking practice. And industrially, the Editdroid represents yet another attempt to cross-media verticals and practice a form of technological entrepreneurialism glamorized, to this day, in post-industrial neoliberal societies. A sense of promise, opportunity, and individual initiative likely contributed to the decision of a famous filmmaker to enter into hardware sales (Lucas), an award-winning ad man to try computer animation and game design (Abel), and a toy maker and cel animator to roll the dice on their own game (Bluth and Dyer). And for each the videodisc was the necessary catalyst to prompt this expansion.

THE POLITICAL ECONOMY OF THE
INTERACTIVE VIDEODISC

Based on the wealth of these contextual examples, I hope that it is clear that *Dragon's Lair* should not be dismissed as simply an aesthetically limited execution of interactivity but should be framed as a discursively symptomatic text illustrative of an uncertain moment where inventors and designers were projecting desires onto the reflective surface of videodiscs. The game then is not bad interactivity, but a productive example and condensation of many of the proliferating discourses around interactivity, its meaning, its function, and its purpose. In his assessment of the term, Lev Manovich (2001) called interactivity a myth. Here the theorist used the term myth to denote falseness, suggesting that many of the stated hallmarks of interactivity concerning user activity and critical awareness were already conceptually present in pre-digital art. However, myth has other definitions equally applicable. Myth also refers to powerful explanatory stories that accumulate meaning through repetition. The historical discussion and production around interactivity described throughout this chapter, I argue, can be read in this second manner, as discourse amassed shaping, directing, and competing over the concept. A similar method is suggested in Greg Smith's (1999) discussion of the emergence of the CD-ROM, in a section entitled "The fantasy of interactivity" (9). Smith uses the term fantasy to underscore the insubstantiality of the concept that "seems to have no central definition" and the malleability of the term to accommodate all the promises of designers, marketers, and writers overeager to articulate the separation of that medium from so-called old media. Although Smith's intention seems to have been to dispel these discussions as "hyperbolic rhetoric" (13) and use fantasy, like Manovich's "myth" in a mostly pejorative sense, as in mere fantasy, I argue instead that the notion of interactivity as a bundle of a conflicted, uncertain promises, realized or not, rational or irrational, is a historically productive. In fact, Huhtamo (1999) argues that the history of media technologies is best achieved precisely through charting this "rhetoric" as discursive inventions, some of which were built, many others that were simply proposed and some of which were adopted, many others that were spectacular failures. Huhtamo further proposes a method of media archeology in which historian examines how recurring discourses in the form of motives, hopes, and promises "have been imprinted on specific media machines and systems in different historical contexts, contributing to their identity in terms of socially and ideologically specific webs of signification" (223). In this final section, I will begin to chart some of these webs of signification around interactivity, considering such basic questions as why it was pursued, what it was imagined to be, how it was to be used, and how specifically it fit into its larger political-economic context. In other words, what were the ideological imperatives that informed this historical pull toward discursive emergence of interactivity in media technology as well as the individuals and firms that produced them and the users, or subjects, that they imagined using them.

Several very important examples of media studies model such a historical method wherein the invention, introduction, and adoption of new media are overwritten and overdetermined by intersecting discourses. Lynn Spigel (1992), in her examination of the introduction of the TV set into the postwar U.S. home, used evidence of popular media and advertising imagery to trace how the presence of that new object was used to articulate powerful notions of feminine domesticity and the specular condition of the 1950s housewife. Similarly, William Boddy (2004) investigated a series of uncertain moments of media change and device adoption using industrial press and, again, advertising material to demonstrate how these pivotal moments in media device history are used to re-assert deeper structures of gender hierarchy and national identity. And, closer to our example, Michael Newman (2017) unpacked the case study of the integration of videogames into the U.S. home at a moment in which notions of masculinity and domesticity were being rehearsed through popular and advertising imagery surrounding these new devices. Carly Kocurek (2015), similarly, had already used popular images of arcade gaming to investigate how early gaming subcultures were gendered male. In all these instructive examples, the authors trace the meaning and significance of new media devices by examining the discourses around them explaining, demonstrating, and defining them, mostly through popular media representations in other formats. A similar project could be constructed studying how videodiscs were positioned in the many popular articles and advertisements promoting their commercial arrival. But in the following section, I will expand these methodological examples instead by incorporating a new set of evidences, scientific papers and patent records, and considering how each does similar discursive work of situating inert technological objects into culturally framed uses.

In 1976 Johannes Mes, a researcher from the electronics firm Philips, earned a patent for his "Information carrier having addressed information tracks." The patent was the first to suggest the use of a disc medium to store, on spiralized lines, a combination of audio-visual signals for display on NTSC monitors with data dumps, in this case referred to as addresses, stored in the horizontal and vertical flyback periods of the traditional TV set's CRT tube. In response to this initial invention, the period from 1973, when Philips first filled Mes's patent, to 1985, in which Sony and Philips released their popular CD format, was an experimental phase wherein videodiscs received relatively little adoption but accumulated a wealth of speculation in the form of technical and legal documents. Ultimately, why the videodisc floundered in this period is less interesting than the sheer abundance of hypothetical videodisc systems, more talked about than used, more dreamed about than implemented. And the specific dream that many of these virtual inventions hovered around was the social utility of interactivity itself.

It is a truism of SF criticism that narratives about the future are about the present. Similarly, technical invention and innovation, as another form of future-directed writing, can be read as responding to the crises of the contemporary moment. In Thomas Streeter's (2010) examination of the growth of microcomputer, the author tracked the immense proliferation of both these devices themselves and theorization around them, finding both to be significantly conterminous with the neoliberal celebration of individualized entrepreneurialism, a worldview and way of being that the microcomputer both inhabited and enabled. Similarly, I argue that the blossoming of speculation around the videodisc and other interactive TV systems echoed its own series of interrelated social crises posed by the economic downturn of the 1970s and 1980s, the concomitant blame heaped on so-called institutional failures, and the eventually proposed neoliberal fixes. The broad notion is that at this historical moment the traditional project of subject formation and social reproduction, as understood by critical theory, in the United States was faltering, resulting in supposed inefficiency and failure in sectors as diverse as business, geopolitics, and health. Implicitly acknowledging these reputed crises, inventors posed videodiscs as part of a solution involving that technology's ability to better accommodate individual choice and organizational agility and, therefore, address these pressing social concerns. In other words, the concept of interactivity here was addressed not simply as technological advancement or aesthetic innovation, but is very much posed as a larger component of the neoliberal reconfiguration of social institutions and subjects, constituting the beginnings of a new kind of disciplinary mechanism increasingly essential to social control.

Surprisingly, the social institution most frequently posed as in the direst need of the specific capabilities of the interactive videodisc was not necessarily one traditionally associated with media. Speculation on the function and purpose of interactivity arrived at a time when the discussions of "failing public schools" was reaching a crescendo, and engineers imagined emerging TV technologies as possible fixes. In 1983, the U.S. Department of Education produced an alarmist report entitled, *A Nation at Risk: The Imperative for Education Reform*, in which the authors attached notions of slackening industry and perceived ebbing of geopolitical confidence to educational performance. The report reads:

> The risk is not only that the Japanese make automobiles more efficiently than Americans and have more government subsidies for development and export.

It is not just that South Koreans recently built the most efficient steel mill, or that the American machine tools, once the pride of the world are being displaced by German products. It is also that these developments signify a redistribution of trained capability. Knowledge, learning, information, and skilled intelligence are the new raw materials of international commerce. . . . If only to keep and improve on the slim competitive edge we retain in world system, we must dedicate ourselves to the reform of the education system for the benefit of all. (6–7)

Astute readers will notice several bugbears of neoliberal critique present in the short excerpt: competition itself is posed as sacrosanct, direct government involvement in industry is cited as inhibitive, and the importance of all forms of human endeavor are gauged by their possible effect on commerce. And although the report was subsequently attacked for inaccuracy and its failure to acknowledge geographical changes that exacerbated structural inequalities in public education, the report's central premise that "our society [was] presently being eroded by a rising tide of mediocrity" was and continues to be an influential one. In fact, the premise of educational failure coupled with economic, social, and political risk became the unlikely premise and justification for many inventors exploring videodiscs and interactive TV. Videogame pioneer Ralph Baer (1986) stated it most clearly in the introduction to his patent for a "Video disc program branching system" in which the inventor wrote,

advancing technology has improved the quality of life of persons in today's society; however, it has also required that citizens thereof become more knowledgeable in more areas. This requirement necessitates that the educational process be similarly advanced and that better learning tools become available to educators. (1)

Baer and his contemporaries imagined the value of interactivity as a fix for the retrospectively presumed passivity of education, which another contemporary DOE report called "one of the greatest challenges facing higher education" (Involvement ... 1984, 23). Many of the contemporary videodisc and interactive technical documents, such as Dale Rodesch's (1983) "Interactive system and method for the control of video play back devices"[11] as well as Dirk Kreon and Klaas Robers's (1984) "Device for interactive video playback," specifically echo this concern by citing education as the preferred embodiment, and nearly all like inventions include education as at least a potential use of the device. Although documents differ on precisely how this technology was to fix education, most refer to the twin capabilities of frame address, which allows for freeze frame, instant replay, and random access, as well as multiplexing to amend a more qualitatively rich activity for students. These capabilities, in turn, were presumed to allow for a screen experience that was more adaptive, responsive, and individualized. In Mes's (1976) own discussion of the videodisc as an ideal "teaching machine," the inventor touted his disc's ability to house a "program [that] can be adapted to the quality of the pupil's answers, thus automatically calling forth an adapted sequence of images" (5). Similarly, in Michel Mathieu's (1977) influential SMPTE article, the author stated, in his own discussion of the videodisc's "major impact on the education environment," that "the possibility of branching among various chains of sequences, using the capability of numerically associating one frame with several others, permits the lessons to be adjusted to the ability of the pupil" (83).

Regardless of the ultimate and likely limited effect of videodiscs and interactive TV on education at this moment, I argue that it is no coincidence that the ideal of the active student gained new purchase in techno-education policy at the same moment that these inventions and their hypothetical uses proliferated. I argue that their confluence points to largescale efforts to reconfigure the ideological work of subject formation in the wake of the political-economic crises cited above and the creation of a neoliberal subject. In his landmark investigation of social reproduction, Louis Althusser (2006) famously cited education and teaching as the ideological state apparatus most responsible for the constitution of subjects used to everyday's repetitive rituals, comfortable with being slotted into interposed roles of exploiter and exploited, and interpolated into an eternally imaginary relationship with social reality. During the 1970s, academics grafted these ideas onto notions of mediated experience, a theoretical innovation often dubbed spectatorship. These theorists used Althusser's notion of reproduction, along with its tragic pupils, and applied it to both the physical arrangement of bodies and the manipulation of erotic and narrative desire in film consumption, typically understood as passive. However, just as the active student became a vital corrective to instructional practice, the central theory of film spectatorship was quickly eroded by empirical, historical, and critical reappraisals of media viewers and their activity (see Mayne 1993), contemporaneously (it is no accident) with technical strides toward so-called interactivity. Instead, film and media studies began to understand users in a frame similar to new active students, as adaptive, responsive, individual, or in a word, interactive. Simply put, I am suggesting that the idealized subject of all these fugued discourses, including the invention and promotion of new devices, drew strength and ideological weight from one another.

What was likely not immediately clear to many of these writers across disciplines was how this new active subject was, in its own way, a product of material production and a site of social reproduction. The transition to this neoliberal subject was expertly diagnosed in Giles Deleuze's (1992) incisive "Postscript on the Societies of Control." In this work, Deleuze outlines what he sees as a great transition from what he calls societies of enclosures where bodies are disciplined in specific time-places. The difference, for the theorist, between classrooms, movie theaters, factory floors and even living rooms is minimal as each operates on its human participants by setting schedules, establishing boundaries, prescribing roles, and minimizing feedback. Deleuze then suggests that by the end of the twentieth century, a new model of social organization emerged in which control is managed not through sameness (from rote memorization in teaching to routinized formula in the industrialized culture industries) but through unique activity or experience and in which humans are not molded into structural roles but are incentivized to become "dividuals" able to move, choice, and act freely. So-called interactive systems, like videogames, arguably function as part of this ideological project and the creation of the dividual by disavowing the cybernetic operations and mixed temporalities, described in chapter 1, and allowing a user to imagine centrality and agency, in a way not dissimilar to what Christian Metz (1982) has previously described as primary identification with the cinematic apparatus that also centered and flattered a viewer with a sensation of power and authority. Christian Laval and Pierre Dardot (2014), in their own examination of the neoliberal subject, stated that this new dividual "is never reduced to a passive object [but is] an active subject who must participate fully, commit himself utterly, and engage completely in his professional [and leisure] activity" (chapter 9). Or, each participant is freed from the "iron cage of rationality," only to be fitted with an iron cage of self-rationalization. Similarly, the collective editors of a book on the so-called *Participation Condition* (Barney, et al 2016) claim that although the activity solicited in interactive systems is interlaced with promise of social change and transformation, the practice is more often "the most prominent means by which individual and publics (at least in the West) become subjects and inscribe themselves in social order" (x). In each of these characterizations, neoliberal society, individual activity, desire, and choice are squared with productivity. All these theorists then contend that power and hierarchy reproduce themselves not through techniques of direct discipline, uniformity, and standardization, but precisely through individual liberalization. If this is true, then a critic should be able to identify the emergence of new and changed social institutions and cultural forms working to facilitate this new and unexpected ideological project.

Although *Dragon's Lair* is not a "teaching machine" in the traditional sense of the term, it can be situated along with its contemporary (proposed) educational machines in regard to its subject effects, specifically in instructing users how to interject themselves into pre-recorded media long before this activity became the political-economic imperative it is today. In this conception the game becomes symptomatic of a much larger attempt to use the idea of interactivity to retrain spectators into users. Admittedly, the student-spectator was only ever a critical abstraction. And admittedly, people actively interacted with screens in the manner described across history. What is important is the new conception of screen interaction, concomitantly along with new ideas of textual construction along with physical and psychical arrangements of humans and machines, took on a productive urgency across interlocking disciplines. Machines like *Dragon's Lair* and Baer's proposed teaching machine signal the beginning of this transition, using the very stuff and textual forms of old media to facilitate a move into a new interactive screen relation, albeit extremely limited with regards to today's technical expectations. Moreover, they can act as a genealogical starting point for the neoliberal interactive subject, which moved from an experimental and redemptive mood to a ubiquitous and mandatory one today. While individual choice, activity, and desire were once posed as correctives to media production (and education) and offered as utopian innovation, digital surveillance, cheap information storage, and robust analytic tools have transformed user interactivity, and it's the data tracings, to the primary natural resource of the largest, most dominant firms in the global economy. *Dragon's Lair* is then an artifact of transition and a site to reconsider the political-economic urgency of interactivity. In this sense, *Dragon's Lair* is not simply a game but an opening gambit in the exchange of traditional screen entertainment for user data, a transaction that now dominates leisure hours and empowers oversized new media firms.

However, what we have not addressed is how the game specifically encourages interaction. In other words, it is all well and good to build an interactive system, by why would someone want to use it? Morningstar (1983) already suggested that it is the long-standing relationship with Mickey Mouse that tricked EPCOT visitors to learn, play, and eventually want new information technology. *Dragon's Lair*, again as a teaching machine, similarly teaches interaction by borrowing imagery and narrative elements, along with the anxieties and desires each provokes, from sword-and-sorcery fantasy, which is the topic of the final chapter.

NOTES

1. Operation of the Worldkey is archived at https://youtu.be/kM2lgMitoVY
2. Some of these games are archived at https://youtu.be/cZJx-KIjL5w
3. Theorist Jean Baudrillard famously interpreted Disneyland's hyperbolic fantastic landscape as a symptomatic assurance that a zone of non-fantasy, brute nature, or the "real" still existed outside its gates. A similar interpretation could be applied to EPCOT whose overwhelming preoccupation with new technology similarly could reassure visitors that a zone of human life free of increasingly intrusive technology still exists.

4. Notably, Lee had contributed programming work to *Dragon's Lair* earlier in his career.

5. To be fair, Best also devotes several passages in the patent to describe another, alternate use of his invention: the facilitation of virtual conversations between users and famous historical persons simulated through the device.

6. The preferred embodiment for Baer's invention was, unsurprisingly, an educational machine.

7. Ironically, slit scan and streaking were two effects that Abel and his employees were known for previously popularizing.

8. The "Play to Win" campaign went on to win two Clios, one for best beverage ad and one for best international campaign.

9. The "Changing Pictures" commercial won Clios for both cel animation and graphics.

10. Mathieu's (1977) article on the videodisc had already marked film editing as being an ideal use for the recording medium and its frame address capability.

11. Rodesch even illogically used the educational frame to describe the appeal of his video gambling machines calling them "instructional tools" for teaching players how to play blackjack (*San Bernardino Sun* 1976).

Chapter 4

Dragon's Lair

The Fantasy

In their book on fantasy in film, Jacqueline Furby and Claire Hines (2012) briefly mention a cycle of so-called sword-and-sorcery films in the early 1980s only to dismiss them as mostly all "lookalikes" (29). The authors further describe these works as "fantasy as formula," containing stock characters, conflicts, and plots. These films' reliance on this formula, which is "extremely narrow, prescriptive, and fixed in form," places them beyond critical appreciation and positions them as bad objects in contradistinction to more expansive uses of the fantasy in film that the authors spend the rest of their manuscript analyzing at length. *Dragon's Lair* arrived at the zenith of this cycle, a revival of sword-and-sorcery that spread across not only motion pictures—*Excalibur* (1981), *Heavy Metal* (1981), *Beastmaster* (1982), *Conan the Barbarian* (1982), *Dragonslayer* (1983), *Fire and Ice* (1983), *Conan the Destroyer* (1985), *Red Sonja* (1985)—but also experienced a resurgence in literature—mostly in the writings of Samuel Delany, Michael Moorcock, and Joanna Russ, among others—exploitation in comic books—*Conan the Barbarian* (beginning in 1970), *Den* (beginning in 1972), *Warlord* (beginning in 1976), *ElfQuest* (beginning in 1978), *Arak, Son of Thunder* (beginning in 1981), and *Amethyst, Princess of Gemworld* (beginning in 1983)—in adaptation in arcade videogames—*Gauntlet* (1985), *Ghosts'N Goblins* (1985), *Black Tiger* (1987)—adaptation in emerging computer games—*Alkabeth: World of Doom* (1980) and *Wizardry* (1981)—exposure on television—*Thundarr, the Barbarian* (1980–1981) *Masters of the Universe* (1983–1985), *Dungeons & Dragons* (1983–1985)—usage in music—through the lyrics, cover art, and graphics of many heavy metal acts of the time such as Dio and Manowar—and a dominating presence in the then-emerging pen-and-paper role-playing games—such as *Dungeons & Dragons* (first sold in 1974) and its many iterations and imitators. The sheer expansiveness of the form's application, demonstrated in this abbreviated list, suggests the dismissal of sword-and-sorcery as simply rote formula might be too dismissive and might present an obstruction to a deeper understanding of the graphic form, the visual surface, and the narrative elements that *Dragon's Lair* used to instruct, guide, and prompt its users, as well as the broader cultural context from which they were adapted. These texts, for a brief window nearly ubiquitous across all of popular culture, drew excessively upon the strange seedbed of the work of a relatively small set of authors associated with early twentieth-century pulp magazines, writers such as Fritz Leiber (reputedly the coiner of the phrase sword-and-sorcery itself), Robert E. Howard, and Clark Ashton Smith. The original short stories by these authors themselves freely repurposed elements from pre-print fantasy traditions such as myth, legend, and fairy tale, along with details pulled from historical chronicles of medieval and ancient societies, in order to cast them into swashbuckling adventure stories in line with the expectations of their pulp editors and audiences. And while the collective project of their work, alternatively called sword-and-sorcery, weird fiction, or low fantasy,[1] may have been a formula, the significance of the formula's revival, and in some cases revision, during the 1970s and 1980s is not at all self-evident.

Many prominent scholars of fantastic tales—from Claude Levi-Strauss to Jack Zipes—have insisted that it is the how and the why of the re-telling of tales that should matter most to the researcher and not the novelty of the story.[2] In this spirit, this chapter will situate *Dragon's Lair* within the sword-and-sorcery revival and ask what precisely it and its contemporary texts drew from this tradition. First, I will consider how the game adapted several of the hallmark textual features that set sword-and-sorcery apart from other fantasy traditions, specifically their glamorization of adventuring protagonists, gothic settings, and morbid and gruesome mood. Second, I will, at the same time, suggest how these recycled elements place this revival within its broader political-economic context, namely the emergence and solidification of the neoliberalist worldview. I argue that *Dragon's Lair* and its intertexts used sword-and-sorcery as a particular form of fantasy to both stimulate and rationalize participation in interactive technical systems and to craft a neoliberal subject whose thoughts, desires, and actions align with ideological priorities. The manipulation of desire to facilitate active participation in interactive systems is, of course, the central premise of much critical analysis of new media writ large, but in *Dragon's Lair* we can decode and analyze an early attempt to achieve this mandate by operationalizing a prior cultural form with its own logic, meaning, and legitimacy. But first, I provide an overview of the notion of the neoliberal subject and its relationship to videogames as a medium.

VIDEOGAMES AND THE NEOLIBERAL SUBJECT

Over the past several decades, contemporaneous with the sword-and-sorcery revival, critical theorists have gravitated toward the concept of neoliberalism as a catchall to describe a set of macro-priorities of global actors as well as the micro-logical symptoms played out in the management of so-called everyday life. As the narrative goes, a series of interlocking crises in the later twentieth century converged to de-legitimate post-industrial capitalism: economic, thanks to a downturn in productivity in the West; technological, thanks to the disruptive introduction of information technologies; and social, thanks to dissatisfaction with industrial labor and its ideological counterpart, mass culture. The result was a new connected set of policies and lived norms Luc Boltanski and Eve Chiapello (2018) called "a new spirit of capitalism" coordinated, as David Harvey (2005) bluntly put it, "to re-establish the conditions of capital and to restore the power of economic elites" (19). Briefly, the "liberalism" in neoliberalism suggested minimizing perceived forms of direct government control would maximize individual freedom at the same time that it would, in turn, unleash the positive effects of market rationality and competition, both freed from supposed interference. Practically, what this worldview resulted in was a set of similarly intentioned strategies to relieve or remove government oversight of social action: privatization, that is the re-categorization of public goods as private property; financialization, the absorption of more and more human activity into growing, complex, centralized markets; de-unionization, as collective bargaining was posed as tampering with individualized competition; deregulation, the removal of (selected) government protectionist and social welfare measures; and a cultural enshrining of the individual entrepreneur as the lived, idealized embodiment of these principles. Political-economic critiques have exposed this worldview as both internally inconsistent, as in the example of firms preaching deregulation yet depending on disavowed nationalized privilege in both domestic and global markets, and contrary to its own intentions, as the fetishization of freedom has only exacerbated unfreedom through both the widening of economic disparity, the consolidation of cultural and information power into fewer, concentrated hands, and the increasing degradation of the natural environment—all direct consequences of neoliberalist policy and action. So, how does such a lousy system persist?

The perpetuation of contradictory social systems through infrastructural, cultural rationalization has long been the preoccupation of critical theory beginning with Marx and Engels. Twentieth-century critical theorists used this basic model, with increasing sophistication, to characterize the precise mechanism whereby culture translates social contradiction into individual rationality, or how the mode of production also manages to produce exactly the type of human agents that it needs to go on. Louis Althusser's influential model of reproduction suggested that social institutions, which he gave the purposeful, machinic moniker apparatus, imprinted individuals with imaginary relationships with social reality, constituting them as normative subjects. Expanding upon this model, Michel Foucault theorized an all-pervasive biopower monitoring not only humans' position with industrial hierarchy but also their minute more forms of behavior and action. In this model, subjects are not just inertly interpellated into identificatory transcendental subject positions, but are disciplined into docile, productive bodies. And Giles Deleuze, in turn, expanded upon this model suggesting that social order is reproduced by accessing and organizing the zone of affect, constituting humans as, in the author's terminology, bodies without organs intermittently attached to desiring machines (for example, videogames) to facilitate, order, and exploit flows of affect itself (desire, emotion, attention, or the theorist's commonly used term, intensity). This drastically truncated lineage serves to demonstrate the broad outlines of the critical theory of subject creation, but what it does not explain is how these theories might modulate with respect to particular cultural forms, particular texts, or particular historical encounters. Such a nuance can be traced by considering the relationship of videogames, as an emerging medium, to their own political-economic context.

It is no coincidence, as the phrase goes, that videogames became a significant cultural form in the moment of neoliberalism's ascendency, and many writers in videogame studies have interrogated whether the medium is doing the ideological work of subject creation and social reproduction as suggested by the above authors and their many followers. In a piece deploying Foucault's concept of governmentality, Andrew Baerg (2009) considers how digital games as a whole have "conducted the conduct of man." The article more specifically echoes and updates the central claim of T. W. Adorno and Max Horkheimer's work on the so-called culture industry in that, just as the theatrical motion picture was described not as a break from industrial labor but it's essential counterpart, Baerg similarly finds universal categories of gaming as undergirding neoliberal rationality. According to Adorno and Horkheimer, hallmarks of Classical Hollywood filmmaking, as a creative practice and industrial process, such as routinization, repetition, and interchangeability, mirrored the rhythm and structure of protoypical factory labor, revealing an aesthetic experience cut to the measure of the mode of production. Baerg points to near universal elements of classic videogames as doing similar ideological work. According to the author the "multidimensional pathfinding" (122) of videogames, that is their affordance of circumscribed user choice felt as freedom, mirror neoliberal preoccupation with free choice and particularly market freedom, and the recurrence of "calculative rationality" (123), that is, the user's constructed priority for accumulating and managing resources (points, lives, turns, ammo, etc.), mirrors the financialization of all social behavior, a particular malignant symptom of neoliberalism. While Baerg's observations are broadly compelling, they lack the specificity of articulating the precise connection of individual games to political-economic determination. Several scholars have taken up precisely this work using individual texts to clarify this relation. Gerald Voorhees (2012) in his examination of *Mass Effect 2* (2011) demonstrated how that game's use of both dialogue and tactical combat mechanics communicated what the author refers to as "neo-liberal multiculturalism," that is respecting of racial difference only insofar as it enhances economic value and/or technocratic productivity. Alfie Bown (2017), in his book of critical interpretation of contemporary videogames, singles out the farm simulator *Stardew Valley* (2016) as a game that romanticizes idyllic pastoral retreat embodying the rugged individualism, anti-communalism, and manipulated nostalgia recurrent in neoliberal rationality. And, more recently, Patrick Jagoda (2020), in his criticism of *Death Stranding* (2019), depicted that game as a celebration of networked individualism through its entrepreneurial messenger protagonist who takes on great personal risk to the ultimate enrichment of his faceless network employer, a condition echoing tody's gig workers from Uber drivers to aspiring YouTubers. These three later writers collectively suggest how the textual elements of specific videogames, from design affordances and limitations to narrative ingredients of storyworld and character, can be decoded with regard to political-economic context. In the following, I will examine the sword-and-sorcery informed visual surface of *Dragon's Lair*, isolating elements of character, space, and mood to consider how the game, and its use of fantasy, can be decoded, too, as a particular product of neoliberal cultural production.

In the next section, I am not suggesting that the original sword-and-sorcery writers were predicting or critiquing a subsequent formation of social existence, although it is interesting to note that these works were written under conditions that we can anachronistically call precarious, that is freelanced and for-hire. Instead, I am suggesting that in the sword-and-sorcery revival of which *Dragon's Lair* was a part, creators drew on the elements that had become culturally resonate, that made the source material malleable for conversion into works reinforcing neoliberal rationality. Many of the macrological political-economic transitions sketched above have resulted in the creation of a new idealized subject, according to critical theorists, imbued with a recurrent set of logics, practices, and desires. Christian Laval and Pierre Dardot (2014) condensed many of these themes into their work on the so-called neoliberal subject whom the authors claimed exhibits enterprise individuality, embraces all-encompassing risk, and accepts personal responsibility for social instability. Examining contemporary business literature, the authors found these character traits as the descriptive and prescriptive measure of a productive (in the Foucauldian sense) individual. By enterprise individuality, Laval and Dardot describe active beings who behave with initiative, who are less reliant on large organizational structures, and who imagine themselves as their own for-profit firm, or enterprise. Moreover, for these actors, all elements of life become assets for potential economic gain: social bonds are replaced with networks of potential collaborators and non-work modes of life are eclipsed by so-called boundaryless careers. The enshrinement of competition and market freedom among neoliberal prophets and apologists equally manifests in business and self-help literature has promoted the resurgence of a kind of rugged individualism, a reduction in the vitality of communal benefit, and the normalization (if not glamorization) of lone risk takers whose publicity and lifestories become one of the major sources of support and justification of the neoliberal worldview. The removal of organizational or social support, however, exposes individuals to great uncertainty, and the ideal neoliberal subject integrates this uncertainty into their everyday existence taking upon themselves, for example, moonlighting gigs, responsibility for re-skilling, and otherwise staying ever vigilant for some alternative life plan when structural forces make one's current one untenable.

While there is no direct one-to-one correlation to these idealized traits and their enactment by subjects, *Dragon's Lair*'s sword-and-sorcery elements can be pulled apart to reveal it as a specific textual machine for subject creation. Specifically, the game's narrative-visual surface presents a way of being, through the figure of the derring-do adventurer hero, a way of moving, through the imperiled dungeon crawl settings, and a way of feeling, through the game's morbid, nihilistic mood. First, I will examine the sword-and-sorcery protagonist as one imbued with individual initiative, dangerous weakness, and immense power. Although the textual construction of a narrative's nominal main protagonist is not certainly the only site to imagine social reproduction at work, it is a significant one. This, I argue, is particularly true in videogames like *Dragon's Lair* which use avatars to rationalize, guide, and compel user thoughts and actions.

"WHAT IS LIFE BUT GREED IN ACTION?"—SWORD-AND-SORCERY'S ADVENTURING HERO

Because of the hybrid nature of *Dragon's Lair*'s construction, the characterization of its protagonist, Dirk the Daring, equally both an observed protagonist and an active avatar, can be read using the tools of both film and videogame analysis. Classical filmed characters, as condensations of narrative information, can be constructed through, among other elements, the accretion of what is outwardly shown, what is subjectively communicated, and what is directly said—or through performance, point-of-view, and dialogue. The performance of Dirk is, in a word, exaggerated. Dirk is depicted in the style of classic slapstick animation, relying on overactive, artistically elongated limbs to emphasize action and accompanying plastic facial features to exaggerate emotion. Although playthroughs vary in the depiction vary in the depiction, a majority of game footage uses Dirk's limber body and rubber face (see fig. 4.1), enhanced by Bluth's previously discussed commitment to full animation, to communicate shock, peril, and surprise, reactions that are often amended with audible whooping or whelping in the game's audio. The sum total of these gestures suggests a character excessively pliable and vulnerable. However, in the rare instance in which Dirk properly unsheathes his sword, the deftness and accuracy of his swings conversely demonstrate skill and strength, as in his successfully played duel with the Lizard King or his disemboweling of the Giddy Goons. In other words, there is a visual contradiction in Dirk's performance as almost foolishly inept and physically dominant, a contrast arguably necessary to articulate mastery of the game to a user. Classical filmmaking grammar typically uses highly conventionalized sequences to denote character thought or inclination, usually dubbed point-of-view structures. Because of the puzzle-like design of *Dragon's Lair* users rarely see a screen absent of Dirk himself, prohibiting the edited sequences used to imply both a character's virtual optical position as well as their internal disposition (see Branigan 1984). However, in the game's final room, *Dragon's Lair* unexpectedly integrates cutaway close-ups, subjectively but

Figure 4.1 Dirk's Rubber Face in *Dragon's Lair* (2017). *Source*: Screenshot Captured from the Digital Leisure PS4 Port.

not optically motivated, of the abducted Princess Daphne oohing and ah-ing, underscoring the erotic drive of the protagonist as well as the identifying user. In the game's attract mode, *Dragon's Lair* plays a short video of select game scenes over which a portentous voice-over is played. The aural description offers a direct and concise account of Dirk as a "valiant knight" on a quest to save a "fair princess." The brevity of the sequence, necessary in part to maximize space on the game's videodisc, relies on the cultural salience of fantasy character types and their intertextual motivations to communicate meaning. Arguably, the overly familiar story relayed in the introduction even invokes the possibility of ironic readings. Perhaps Dirk is not so very "valiant," as suggested in contradictory moments such as the conclusion of the Lizard King's room in which Dirk is depicted as slyly grabbing a handful of loose gold coins before continuing on through the next door—notably the coins are rendered in backlit animation giving the gold a glowing lure (see fig. 4.2).

The voice-over, too, belies artistic choice in the shaping of the character of Dirk whose intention is described as a quest, a form of narrative usually centered on single individuals, and whose goal is not couched in social motivations (i.e., save the kingdom, restore peace, win a war, etc.) but only to fulfill delayed erotic drive, revealed and then denied in the game's final image of Dirk and Daphne's embrace. In sum, the game uses filmic codes of characterization to represent Dirk as a protagonist that is equal parts weak and powerful, and as defined through individualized pursuits of personal desire. Of course, this description could be equally apt of most early gaming protagonists; Pac-man seems to be motivated by personal greed and quickly

Figure 4.2   Dirk Quickly Snatching Some Gold in *Dragon's Lair* (2017). *Source:* Screenshot Captured from the Digital Leisure PS4 Port.

vacillates between pursuit and pursued during play. However, *Dragon's Lair* demonstrates how the symbolic resources of sword-and-sorcery are used to communicate and rationalize this combination of traits.

The work of characterization in videogames is complicated by the playability of the avatar; however, the procedural elements of gameplay in *Dragon's Lair* often work in a manner redundant with Dirk's outward representation. Petri Lankoski (2010) has examined how game designers use characters' narrative goals and behaviors as indications and incentives to play "in character." On a simple level, this is true of *Dragon's Lair* in which, as in the case of many arcade videogames, users must minimally identify with the desirability of the diegetic end goal (perhaps ironically) in order for the game to continue. Avatars also act as shapers of intention not only through implied character psychology but also, as James Newman (2002) put it, as "sets of available capabilities and capacities" encoded in system hardware and software. Game design, further, filters these capabilities into preferred or otherwise incentivized forms of action. In *Dragon's Lair*, a user directs Dirk with eight-way joystick and a lone, tantalizing button denoted "sword." Despite its prominent display on cabinet panel art which depicts Dirk with his weapon drawn and the aural description of the character as a "valiant knight," the avatar's capability to use a sword is rarely the correct choice to the game's obstacles. All told, only roughly 35 of the game's decision points are properly resolved with the sword button, while approximately 157 other points must be solved by joystick manipulation, or colloquially movement. Thus, to play "in character," the game's very design suggests that evasion, running, and other movement must be prioritized over physical force or outward violence for the game to continue. For example, a user must accomplish six timed evades before drawing their sword against the Lizard King, and seven times before attacking the titular Dragon in the game's final room. In many cases, a user must avoid using the sword altogether, leaving the haunted crypt, the stairwell, and the snake room before the onscreen enemies are fully vanquished, and fleeing from the lava-men before ever striking a single sword blow (see fig. 4.3).

I argue that this design choice of presenting an affordance, the sword, and severely tempering its use in play contributes to the specific style of interactivity in the game (as discussed in the previous chapter), and adds to the characterization of Dirk as excessively vulnerable. Moreover, design choices further reinforce this characterization with regards to the game's treatment of health, or vitality, as well as what we can call the overarching "difficulty" of the game. While the cabinet gives individual users multiple tries, each try only allows for one error. Diegetically, this means that with one false move, Dirk dies. Progressing or completing the game necessitates that a user chooses, or more likely memorizes, and performs long sequences of joystick and button combinations which are as long as 12 (in the case of the Lizard King room)

Figure 4.3   Dirk Runs from the Mud Men in *Dragon's Lair* (2017). *Source:* Screenshot Captured from the Digital Leisure PS4 Port.

or 13 depressions (in the case of the underground river room). The length of these play sequences and the dire stakes of the correct responses creates an emergent game experience that outwardly could be described as "difficult" and diegetically read as representing Dirk being somewhat over his head!

This mix of character traits attributed to Dirk, via filmed representation and designed processes, resonate deeply with the conventions of sword-and-sorcery and its then-contemporary revival. In these works, our central protagonists rarely are the fated heroes, the melodramatic lost nobles, or the selfless, chivalric knights-errant of so-called high fantasy variants of the form whose own narratives are informed by their characters' immense in-world ability, their high status in the storyworld, and the clear imperative of their motivations. Instead, the protagonist of sword-and-sorcery more typically occupies roles that prioritize individual desire and personal initiative. They are largely thieves, freebooters, or outsiders whose own desires, and the actions that they inform, put them at odds with their represented social milieus. In a word, they are adventurers. The transition from this earlier high fantasy protagonist to the adventurer is broached by an early text of the sword-and-sorcery revival, John Boorman's *Excalibur*. On the one hand, this film is another re-telling of the King Arthur legend wherein the meekest subject of the realm becomes the ideal leader to unite the scattered kingdoms of Britain, and in which the phallic sword in the stone (the weapon of Arthur's father by way of Freud) is used as an overdetermined image of fate itself. However, the story of Arthur as a selfless redeemer operating via mystical right is narratively bookended by two echoed subplots of desire and hubris, desire led to ruin. In the film's prologue, Uther Pendragon, Arthur's absent father and first king of a united Britain, is overcome with lust and forces the magician Merlin to devise a supernatural trick to allow him to seduce the wife of a rival. Merlin attempts to resist, considering the act as an abuse of power and an affront to social order; however, he relents Uther's will, leading indirectly to the king's demise. And, later in the film, Arthur's knight Lancelot is impaled during a joust during a contest to defend the honor of Queen Guinevere. In response, Arthur demands Merlin use his magics to save the knight's life. Once more, Merlin attempts to resist, calling the act contrary to fate and law—the cause that Lancelot was fighting for was, in the terms of narrative, false—however, he relents to Arthur's will, indirectly leading to this king's own decline, and the decline of the kingdom, too, as his social body. According to the moral economy of the film, each of these consequential actions, born each of forceful will and desire, is emphatically "wrong," leading to the ruination of both the individual actor as well as the entire social system which emanates from each.[3] In this framed narrative construction, film acts as a transitional attempt to bring the sword-and-sorcery protagonist, the adventurer, into a more classical fantasy narrative which, because it ends on a nationalistic, albeit ironic note of the eternal endurance of the realm or the social itself, cannot sustain them. Several other contemporary sword-and-sorcery films wrestled precisely with this conflict by introducing seemingly false protagonists, that is characters who appear as official high fantasy protagonists and who are eventually narratively supplanted by more cunning adventurer, as in both the case of *Dragonslayer* and *Conquest*. The adventurer as protagonist, conversely, has long been part of the literary tradition of sword-and-sorcery since the subgenre's formulation.

Fritz Leiber's recurring sword-and-sorcery characters Fafhrd and the Grey Mouser clearly demonstrate a notable set of fantasy protagonists defined by personal initiative, evasive cunning, and individual desire. The intent of the characters was plainly stated in their initial appearance in a story aptly named "Two Sought Adventure" ([1939] 1970).[4] This story begins en media res as the two protagonists are tracking a treasure map previously stolen by the Mouser. Before infiltrating a temple rumored to hold the treasure, the adventurers stop overnight at a modest farm wherein Mouser marvels at their hosts, in interior monologue, "how can people sleep so near jewels and not dream of them?" (30). The contrast of the scene and Mouser's emphatic incredulousness marks the protagonists as exceptional in their chosen vocation, guided not by routine or duty, like the proprietors of the farm, but the lure of treasure and the "spice" of conflict (26). The characterization of the partners is further pronounced decades later in the story "Ill Met in Lankhmar" ([1970] 1983).[5] In this story, Lebier depicts Fafhrd and the Grey Mouser as literal freelancers, operating as cutpurses outside and independent of a rigid Thieves Guild that occupies the titular setting. The narrative begins as the protagonists rob a mirrored pair of union thieves who are notably described with their bureaucratic titles "Slevyas, master thief candidate . . . [and] Fissif, thief second class" (165). After this burglary, the protagonists occupy a good portion of the rest of the story drinking wine and explaining to one another and to their respective romantic partners, Vlana and Ivrian, why it is not in their best interests to fulfill Fafhrd's blood oath to attack and eliminate the Thieves Guild, much to the derision of Ivrian who projects chivalric motives onto the two thieves. Initially, Ivrian's entreaties fall on deaf ears because Fafhrd and Grey Mouser are characters based on individual desire counterposed to any sense of larger social duty or obligation, a worldview encapsulated by the pair's later antago- nist, Krovas, who succinctly opines, "what is life but greed in action?" (230). Although it is a choice overdetermined by the publishing format of periodical literature, it is notable that for adventurers like Fafhrd and Grey Mouser, or their more famous contemporary Conan the Cimmerian, there is no happy ending. The stereotypical "happily ever after" or eucatastrophe of fairy tales of Tolkeinesque high fantasy that redeems social order is impossible as, for adventurers, there is always another job, another desire to quenched, or from the perspective of the equally freelance sword-and-sorcery writers another story to be paid for. "More later" instead is the conventional end of these stories—most famously articulated in the final spoken line of the film *Conan the Barabarian*: "but that is another story"—and is equally applicable to the often-truncated experience of arcade gaming. So, it is with both "Two Sought Adventure" and "Ill Met in Lankhmar" which conclude with the protagonists, denied their ultimate reward, ambling on to another town and another job.

The construction of the self-interested sword-and-sorcery protagonist became a strong influence on the design of the interlocking gamebooks produced by TSR under the banner of *Dungeons & Dragons* (D&D) and its offshoots during the sword-and-sorcery revival. At first, the comparison of *Dragon's Lair* to D&D might be a surprising one, given that D&D is celebrated as a game with few user boundaries, while *Dragon's Lair* is infa- mous for being the opposite. Yet clearly both share a cultural link through the sword-and-sorcery stories that inform each. In the *Advanced Dungeons & Dragons Dungeon Masters Guide* (1979), author Gary Gygax even included an "Appendix N" that listed many of the original sword-and-sorcery authors, such as Leiber and Howard, as literary antecedents of the game. But I argue the two share not only the cosmetic features of shared imagery—clearly both contain dungeons and dragons—but also the structural elements of character, space, and mood. In the first case, D&D presents a game protagonist, echo- ing the above, as an individual granted physical power, cursed with extreme vulnerability, and animated by singular desire. Several popular histories (see for example Ewalt 2013; Witwer 2015), situate the conception of an individualized war game where participants take on the roles of single-game avatars as the essential innovation of D&D. Recent archival work by Jon Peterson (2020), however, has demonstrated that individualized play was not unique to D&D, and that even among early D&D players the question as to how deeply one was to inhabit this role was hotly debated.[6] However, D&D was clearly one game among others that celebrated individual choice and the decision-making of its adventurer "heroes" and promised users the in-game capacity to make fateful choices and achieve (possibly) their intended results. One of the primary design innovations of D&D was to cloud the promise of this open-ended decision-making through the filter of player character, the role taken on, which winnowed probable decisions into preferred strategies based on game elements such as attributes, which detail a players' physical ability, classes, which list players' professional strategies, and alignment, which outlines players' ethical tendencies. D&D was also uncommon histori-cally among other games for its lack of definitive goal or explicit winning condition. Instead, the individual motivation was given narrative pretense succinctly described in a 1983 version of the game by Gygax and co-creator Dave Arneson and co-author Frank Mentzer: "Day by day you explore the unknown looking for monsters and treasure. The more you find, the more powerful and famous you become" (2). Previous critical work by Aaron Trammel (2018) and Sarah Stang (2020) has convincingly demonstrated how core design decisions of D&D have perpetuated racial and sexual hierarchies in the guise of play. Looking at the core game motivation and the incentiv-ization of so-called experience[7] too reveals how the game accommodates and reproduces other symptoms of neoliberal rationality, specifically the preoccupation with continuous self-improvement and boundless accumula-tion. Matthew Chrulew (2006) called this the "entrepreneurial structure" of D&D whereby "completing their tasks, characters gain experience, treasure, and items, and advance in ability levels, power, and prestige" (148). This improvement is facilitated by another novel game mechanic usually attributed to D&D, experience points, quantifiable reward dispensed for either eliminat-ing enemies in simulated combat or amassing in-world treasure, that bestow players with both narrative and out-of-game awards. Individual adventure modules, or game scenarios, interlock these diegetic, in-world, and non-diegetic, mechanical, motivations conventionally beginning with "rumors" of an infamous monster to vanquish and an accompanying treasure hoard to plunder. For example, in the game book *Tomb of Horrors* (Gygax 1978b), players begin with the knowledge that there is a powerful demi-lich hiding an ancient burial mound flanked by riches, both vehicles for experience accumu-lation. The experience mechanic, then, incentivizes gameplay of individual initiative, risk-taking, and martial combat. In sum, the player is incentivized to become an adventurer.

However, the represented derring-do for sword-and-sorcery's protagonists is equally tempered with their equal vulnerability, weakness, and fallibility. A rather extreme depiction of this convention occurs in Lucio Fulci's *Conquest*. The film begins with a prologue in which the lead character Ilias is gifted a magic bow and is sent on a vague quest by his father to a distant land coded as less developed in the manner, dress, and technology of its inhabitants. Here Ilias runs afoul an evil wizard, Zora, and her savage wolf-henchmen. Thus far, the combination of elements (magic gifts, quests, evil wizards) marks the film to be stereotypical fantasy. But before Ilias can challenge the antagonist, he is surprisingly killed two-thirds into the film's running time, leaving his adopted side-kick, a caveman clad in furs named Mace, to take up the bow and defeat Zora. Short of character death, sword-and-sorcery more generally exposes the weakness and shortcomings of its protagonists. Michael Moorcock's ([1972] 1987) own recurring sword-and-sorcery character Elric of Melniboné is emphatically fragile and, colloquially, strung out: "[Elric] had lived—still lives—thanks to sorcery alone, for he is naturally lassitudiousness and, without drugs, would barely be able to raise his hand from his side for most of a normal day" (5). Even in stories of Fafhrd and Grey Mouser, Leiber frequently presents narrative scenes of what must be called blundering. Both of the previously mentioned Leiber tales end in either failure (the jewels are not recovered) or at best pyrrhic victory (revenge is won, but only at the cost of the lives of the duo's romantic partners). Moreover, throughout most of "Ill Met . . ." the protagonists are engaged in comic folly or error. In order to invade the headquarters of the Thieves Guild, the two adventurers disguise themselves as blind and maimed beggars. The planned subterfuge fools a single "mark" outside of the building but fails to mislead a single occupant that the two encounter within the guildhall, including the guildmaster, Krovas, who demands that they give up their "inexpert acting" (227). While in the headquarters, the thieves also clandestinely spy on the guild's wizard, Hristolomo, and later the story retrospectively reveals that they were not even successful at this skulking but instead that the wizard saw them and gauged them to be beneath suspicion or curiosity. Also, while in the guildhall, Fafhrd and Grey Mouser are surprised to observe that rats can talk—a fact discussed and vehemently denied by the pair earlier in the story—which leaves an eyewitness to the pair's initial theft at the story's beginning. This sequence of Fafhrd and Grey Mouser's initial reconnaissance of the Thieves Guild, itself in part narratively motivated by an excess of wine drinking, repeatedly exposes the ostensible heroes as incredibly inept.

In his own discussion of sword-and-sorcery, Richard Matthews (2011) singles out the formative influence of H. Rider Haggard, another pulp author, who, in his writings, "elevated primitive power and brute force to new importance" (119). Like Haggard, sword-and-sorcery writers typically endow their protagonists, in contrast with the aforementioned vulnerability, with immense physical strength or prowess that is encoded through overwrought depictions and descriptions of the body in action that give the protagonist both the thematic pretense and narrative authority to both exercise this power and commit violence.[8] Preoccupation with the body, or a particularly encoded body, and its capacity for violence also constitutes what George Slusser (2002) calls fantasy's "anthropocentric vision" in which "the human form remains its central presence, its determining icon" (10). This tendency is clear in what is sword-and-sorcery most culturally resonant image, Frank Frazetta's "Conan the Barbarian" (1965). In this oft-produced and oft-parodied painting, the subject, Conan, musculature thickly outlined, stands in visual contrast to the wispy and sketchy death's heads and compositionally on top of a mass strew with unfinished body parts, implying the aftermath of immense violence. Standing alone atop a mound, Conan's nearly naked body, on display, is positioned on the vertex of the image's triangular composition giving redundant prominence to his imposing figure. Frazetta would re-use the same compositional balance and effect in several other often-reproduced Conan and sword-and-sorcery images, such as "Conan the Destroyer" (1971) and "Death Dealer" (1973).

Likewise, Leiber casts his Fafhrd and Grey Mouser as clear masters of violence, and grounds this mastery in the description of their bodies. In "Two Sought Adventure" Leiber introduces his characters with a quick visual assessment of the pair: Fafhrd "[h]is great lean muscles, white skin, copper hair, green eyes, and above all the pleasant yet untamed expression of his massive countenance all hinted at a land of origin colder, rougher and more barbarous than that of Lankhmar" and Mouser "[s]omething about the set of his wiry frame betokening exceptional competence in street fights and tavern brawls" (21). Description of the characters, at this point still unnamed in the story, immediately connects their frame with is potential and capacity to commit violence. Moreover, the narrative authority the pair holds to exercise this capacity is well demonstrated in the structural variation of the events of "Ill Met . . ." After escaping their first bumbling escapade to the Thieves Guild, described above, the story repeats itself depicting the protagonists' return trip to guildhall. However, in this case, the protagonists do not attempt to disguise themselves but instead approach the headquarters with intentions of open confrontation, an act that Fafhrd himself earlier in the same story described as "t'would be insanity to attack the building directly" (194). Nonetheless, the two, are described as receiving very little physical resistance to their incursion while they burn and swipe their way back to wizard Hristolomo whom they violently slay by way of a thrown dagger which "[buries] itself to the hilt in his right eye." (252). What's more, the physical presence, prowess, and power depicted through Fafhrd and Grey Mouser as well as its resultant violence is of a very particular kind, predicated not on magic, in opposition to Hristolomo, or even on social authority, in opposition to the guild itself, but on the simple adeptness and force of their bodies, or in Matthews's terminology primitive power and brute force. And it was this focus on the powerful body which became one of the hallmarks most traded upon in the sword-and-sorcery revival.

The translation of sword-and-sorcery literature into other visual media of the 1980s coincided with a tendency in U.S. action cinema to focus on the male body in extremis, a tendency Susan Jeffords (1994) called "hard body" films. In her analysis, Jeffords examines the recurrence of the image of the white male muscular body as a crystallization of Reaganite philosophies, politics, and economics. Imagined as a collective symbol in response to the perception of national deterioration, the hard body deployed actors such as Arnold Schwarzenegger and Sylvester Stallone as a new identificatory ideal used to narratively defeat a number of conservative bugbears on the geopolitical level—"evil empires," "unfree" states—and the domestic—encroaching bureaucratization and panics over "urban" crime. Indeed, John Milius's *Conan the Barbarian* can be read productively in such an allegorical manner decoding Reaganite themes: a bootstrapping white male raises himself up from nothing (from literal slavery) to become successful, self-employed entrepreneur (a thief, but greed is good) who later dismantles a foreign social order depicted as being dependent on coercive thought control. According to Jeffords, hard body imagery and narratives were also contrasted to the flawed, imperfect "soft body which almost invariably belonged to a woman or person of color," doing the ideological work of reproducing racist and sexist hierarchies articulated to conservative ideals of national solidarity (25). Film critic Robin Wood (2003) applied this same critique directly to *Conan the Barbarian* in much more forceful terms, calling the film's celebration of the powerful white male body a backlash against feminism and a work of overt fascism.

Indeed, to represent the superimposition of physical power and narrative authority, many sword-and-sorcery have drawn upon the semiotics of race and racism. In the creation of his two enduring pulp characters, John Carter of Mars and Tarzan of the Apes, writer Edgar Rice Burroughs, a progenitor of the sword-and-sorcery form, borrowed on the presumed privilege of the white male body to rationalize and enshrine each one's exceptional strength. Upon his arrival to Mars, Carter dominates the Green Martians, mirror-imaged displacements of the American Indians he briefly encounters in the story's first chapter, only because he is an Earth man, and Tarzan likewise dominates the African landscape by virtue of his English royal blood as the heir to Greystoke. Moreover, each character operates in a loaded setting on the edge of implied civilization and its other which, according to Brian Attebery

(1980) doubly marks Burroughs's fiction as ideologically perpetuating a colonialist worldview. The equation of white male power over and above dark-skinned subhumans regrettably survives through the sword-and-sorcery revival in films such as Ralph Bakshi's *Fire and Ice*, itself based on the art and painting of Frank Frazetta. While Burroughs's adventures were deeply informed by physical anthropology and what Mark Jerng (2018) call biological racism, the grounding of quasi-medical theories of racial superiority based on debunked disciplines such as eugenics and phrenology, Robert E. Howard, the creator of Conan, partially complicated these ideas by incorporating notions of then-emerging cultural notions of race. Like Burroughs before him, Howard glorified the white male body while denigrating the black body with harmful stereotypes and deployed a recurring literary motif of blackness itself as coterminous with all that is evil and unholy. In Charles R. Saunders's ([1975] 2011) famous critique of sword-and-sorcery literature, the author rightly accused Howard of participating in "antiblack hysterics," using black characters in a manner that "would have made excellent propaganda for Adolph Hitler" and placing narratives in settings of intentionally fabricated ancient worlds where white racial dominance was unquestioned. Moreover, Howard's Conan stories display a fanatical effort to sort and define his story-world's multitude of racial types by physiognomy (what does Shemite look like?), disposition (how do Stygians behave?), and cultural proclivities (what crafts are the Zamorans known for?), both through direct authorial exposition and through protracted debate and offhand comments of diegetic characters. Through this obsessive cataloguing, Howard apes his contemporary proto-anthropologists, like Henri Louis Morgan and Franz Boas, who argued for the coherence and intellect behind so-called tribal societies, as well as quasi-archeologists like Howard Carter and Hiram Bingham who very publicly promoted the wealth and beauty of ancient societies. These emerging examples of cultural and historical relativism at least tempered the racial hierarchies and colonial conflicts that replay in Howard by way of Burroughs. As a clear example, Jerng points out that in Howard's fiction, the boundaries of so-called civilization and savagery are not isomorphic with constructed whiteness in Conan's setting, Hyborea, as evidenced in the case of the Picts, an ethnical tribe of wild gleaners who had devolved into savagery in the eyes of the other fictional societies of the storyworld. And Conan himself, a character like Burrough's Tarzan and James Fenmoore Cooper's Natty Bumppo, is a fantastic white body imbued with the projected qualities of modernity's constructed other, the savage, and created by an author infamous for his distaste of contemporary everyday life.[9] Several writers associated with the sword-and-sorcery revival attempted to prove that this recurrent racist vision was a bug and not a feature of sword-and-sorcery. Saunders himself contributed the Imaro series ([1981] 2006) which re-cast Tarzan and Conan stories with an African warrior, and Samuel Delany's *Tales of Nevèrÿon* (1979) used a fantastic setting and a Conan-esque protagonist (Gorgik, a warrior and former slave) to tell a complex tale about the relationship of slavery to the emergence of market and cash economies. Despite these significant works, the legacy of these previously sketched intertexts persist in the overdetermined whiteness, patriarchal gaze, as well as the equivalence of bodily excellence and narrative rightness, remains typical of the form and shades even the construction of *Dragon's Lair*. Burroughs and Howard's outward and coded racism haunts the subgenre as a conventionalized infrastructure that then becomes the structurally absent motivation of less thoughtful and even more enlightened executions of sword-and-sorcery.

The interlocking features used in defining the sword-and-sorcery protagonist as it was originally crafted and redrafted in revival interexts, presents a cultural pretext for the possibilities and limitations of *Dragon's Lair*'s game design at the same time as it connects the texts to structural issues of political-economic determination. It should be clear that the game's user (and their avatar) is incentivized and prompted to take initiative, imagine physical power, and accept vulnerability in a manner already outlined in classical and revived sword-and-sorcery texts.[10] These themes resonate with the neoliberal rationality discussed in critical analyses of the era in which a new subject for social order was drafted and whose proclivities were for adventure.

"NEARLY EVERY ROOM IN MY HOUSE IS A TRAP"— SWORD-AND-SORCERY'S PERILOUS SPACES

In his examination of the sword-and-sorcery subgenre, author Michael Moorcock (2004) described it as one that hybridized events of martial action from chivalric romances with the gothic setting. Moorcock expanded on the latter suggesting that works of this form could not be judged with the standards of literary fiction—that is, by the psychological complexity of characters, the intricateness of plotting, or incisiveness of commentary, etc.—but by the richness of their expressive landscapes which "reflect the themes of the stories, amplify or at least compliment the moods of the characters, [and] give added texture and apt symbolism to the narratives" (72). Indeed, many early sword-and-sorcery stories are dominated by their settings in terms of their plots, which are preoccupied with tales of spatial incursion, invasion, or escape; their narration, which often affects a digressional gaze and uncommon focus on space itself; and their conflicts, which typically framing spatial movement as movement in peril. I argue that these lessons of spatial construction, in turn, informed the works of the sword-and-sorcery revival and its frequent use of the so-called dungeon crawl. Below, I will place *Dragon's*

Lair in specific conversation with several works by Howard to elucidate how the game's own image of space participated in this tradition and, ultimately, how its tendencies too reflect the social contradictions of neoliberalism.

The first two shots viewed in any *Dragon's Lair* gameplay makes these antecedents clear. Upon pressing game start, the cabinet screen displays an establishing shot of a dark castle, ringed in modeled purple sky, in a physically illogical state of disrepair, a conventional setting of gothic storytelling. The shot features a canted push-in and planed parallax effect to accentuate a ring of black, spiked briars enclosing the image foreground, signaling the ruin of the scene and the menace it portends (see fig. 4.4). The game immediately frames itself as one of spatial incursion through the slow, virtual push-in shot as well as the aggressive inward run of the avatar through the castle gates in the succeeding shot. Echoing design choices discussed in chapter One, these initial shots pose the setting as the obstacle to be overcome, as the briars partially block the forward, z-axis movement and the slamming gateway portcullises behind Dirk (see fig. 4.5), which actually come between the user and their proxy, suggest a malevolent personification of the castle itself. And, reiterating discussions of *Dragon's Lair*'s particular style of interactivity, these depictions feature a beguiling amount of detail, from the irregular set of castle spires to the minute modeling on its decaying flagstones. These loose observations support both Henry Jenkins's (2004) claim that videogames often use spatial detail to accommodate storytelling and Mark J.P. Wolf's (2012) contention that a preponderance of seemingly minute visual details facilitate the subcreation of fantasy storyworlds and settings. I further argue

Figure 4.4 The Dragon's Castle in *Dragon's Lair* (2017). *Source*: Screenshot Captured from the Digital Leisure PS4 Port.

Figure 4.5   The Portcullis Falls behind Dirk in *Dragon's Lair* (2017). *Source*: Screenshot Captured from the Digital Leisure PS4 Port.

that the techniques of spatial representation echo the aesthetic strategies found in the works of the work of Howard, as well as his contemporaries and later artistic interlocutors.

Howard, through his Conan series, developed a plotting formula recurrent throughout sword-and-sorcery in all media that we can call plots of incursion. By this, I mean that the plots principally focus on the narration of character movement through physical space and the manner in which this movement is waylaid by obstacles of environment or sentient opposition. Howard's "Tower of the Elephant" ([1933] 2020) best lays this formulation bare. This story begins as Conan plainly states his intention, to his fellow rogues, to scale the titular tower and to rob the jewel, "The Heart of the Elephant," rumored to reside within. In order to do so, the protagonist is described as surmounting a series of spatially distributed and increasingly dangerous obstacles. After ascending an initial outer wall Conan's accomplice, Taurus, dispatches a human guard. Scaling a second wall reveals a pack of guard lions, defeated with a dose of poison gas. And after climbing the actual tower, Conan successfully battles a giant spider before descending into a room containing the desired heart. The plot, then, is organized by a single vectorized movement, clearly established at the plot's opening, which is punctuated by a gauntlet of obstacles. Many subsequent Conan stories can be read as more baroque revisions of this core formula. "Rogues in the House" ([1934] 2020) combines a series of incursion into one narrative: Conan escapes prison; both Conan and his accomplice, Murilo, invade the domicile of the wizard Nabonidus; and then all three work together to escape the wizard's dungeon. And Howard's final Conan story, "Red Nails" ([2021] 1939) drastically expands the scope of incursion by presenting its protagonists with a singular, immense walled-in city. The plot of incursion became so synonymous with the character that filmed adaptations of Conan contain elaborate, near pantomime actions scenes mimicking their construction in *Conan the Barbarian*'s theft at the Temple of Set and *Conan the Destroyer*'s invasion of the tower of the wizard Thoth-Amon. Moreover, the plot of incursion became a storytelling template for both sword-and-sorcery contemporaries and revisionist creators. Indeed, both the Leiber stories described above can be understood as incursions: "Two Sought Adventure" depicts the adventurers' attempt to raid a single location; "Ill Met . . ." is also principally built around the ironic juxtaposition of two sallies into the Thieves Guild. And in one of the more interesting variations of this formula, Gorgik, Delany's revision of Conan in *Tales of Nevèryon*, is trapped in an immense castle, the High Court of the Eagles, and nearly dies of starvation not because of physical combat but because of social conflict. Specifically, Gorgik is unable to grasp how to use his social connections in order to secure an invitation to dinner in one of the castle's many halls. Even in this example, the formula of movement through contested space set with obstacles is preserved.

In Howard's plots of incursion, the author frequently punctuates the characters' movement through space with both atemporal expository digressions stuffed with minute detail as well as nested, embodied narrations of deep pasts, both constituting a style of thick description. Although the Conan stories, in terms of technical verbal phrasing, are rendered in an indistinct past there is, I argue, an overwhelming "presentness" to the storytelling as a result of the relatively brief timeline of plotted events ("The Tower . . ." takes place over a single diegetic night), the single-mindedness of motivation (Conan wants to steal the jewel), and the reliance on narrative surprise for both the reader and the characters themselves (Conan is ambushed by the giant spider). Howard, likely borrowing a structural feature common to his infamous colleague and fellow *Weird Tales* contributor H.P. Lovecraft, supplements these present-like tales with nested stories delivered by in-world characters. In "The Tower . . . ," the interstellar, elephant-headed alien called Yogah explains how he came to Earth in time to witness the very ascent of human society followed by the decline of ancient mythical kingdoms of Atlantis and Lemuria, only to be imprisoned by a malevolent sorcerer. In narratological terms, Howard manages to fit story events stretching back to the beginning of time, as well as across the vastness of outerspace, into a plot taking place over one fateful night, and mostly in a single location. Howard also frequently pauses the chronology of his plot events not only to delve into the deep past of the storyworld but also to explore space itself from a disembodied gaze.

"The Tower," in fact, begins with such a reverie recounting an impression of the slum of Arenjun known as the "The Maul":

> Along the crooked, unpaved streets with their heaps of refuse and sloppy puddles, drunken roisterers staggered, roaring. Steel glinted in the shadows where wolf preyed on wolf, and from the darkness rose the shrill laughter of women, and the sounds of scufflings and strugglings. Torchlight licked luridly from broken windows and wide-thrown doors, and out of those doors, stale smells of wine and rank sweaty bodies, clamor of drinking-jacks and fists hammered on rough tables, snatches of obscene songs, rushed like a blow in the face.

Here sensorial data intermingle to provide an impression of place. Later, the tale's timeline halts once more as Conan approaches the Tower and the narration relays a schematic of the environment:

> The shimmering shaft of the tower rose frostily in the stars. In the sunlight it shone so dazzlingly that few could bear its glare, and men said it was built of silver. It was round, a slim perfect cylinder, a hundred and fifty feet in height, and its rim glittered in the starlight with the great jewels which crusted it. The tower stood among the waving exotic trees of a garden raised high above the general level of the city. A high wall enclosed this garden, and outside the wall was a lower level, likewise enclosed by a wall. No lights shone forth; there seemed to be no windows in the tower—at least not above the level of the inner wall. Only the gems high above sparkled frostily in the starlight.

Here, the impassive, disembodied visual assessment informs and supplies the plot of incursions with its field of obstacles. Digressionary focus and thick description, stylistic tendencies in a form known mostly for grim, violent action, reaches an early apotheosis in the work of another *Weird Tales* writer, Clark Ashton Smith's "The Seven Geases" ([1934] 2007). In this story, the protagonist is cursed, robbed of his own bodily volition, and is compelled by a series of malevolent entities to descend deeper and deeper into a series of bizarre, subterranean landscapes. Unable to control his own walking body, the protagonist becomes a blank observer only able to absorb and catalogue his surroundings, essentially becoming a narrative pretense for an extreme example of sword-and-sorcery preoccupation with setting.

Howard's densely wrought spaces are also characterized as zones of perpetual menace and conflict. In "Red Nails," Conan and his accomplice Valeria enter the walled city of Xuchotl and find it absent of all but a grim, internecine war. Exterior descriptions of the space explain that all evidence of commerce, agriculture, or industry that would supply such an immense location was either absent or in ruin. Inside the city, the two encounter several warring groups in the final throes of a death spiral, consumed with eradicating the other and a "determination to die dealing death." The entire city exists only as a battlefield, as Howard relays, "[i]n the miniature world of Xuchotl each handful of feudists was an army, and the empty halls between the castles was the country over which they campaigned." In Howard's plots of incursion, space is fraught with violent ambush and deadly obstacle. The later, colloquially understood as traps, become a significant convention of his writing. "Rogues in the House" provides the most elaborate examples as Nabonidus's lair is ringed by activating a number of trap doors and jets of poison gas. Near the conclusion of the narrative, the wizard frankly boasts, "nearly every chamber in my house is trap." Several of Howard's contemporaries took this impulse even further by literalizing the menace of space through personification. Leiber's "Two Sought Adventure" culminates as the temple which the adventurers intended to raid becomes animated, smashing its tower down toward the protagonists like a fist. Fafhrd and Grey Mouser's suspicion of the initial treasure map and its enticing poems suggest that the entire temple was, in fact, purpose-built as an enormous mousetrap for greedy grave robbers. And in Clark Ashton Smith's "The Ice-Demon" ([1933] 2006), the protagonists are imperiled by a malignant glacier that, protecting its own cache of jewels, projects icicles, chews on intruders with mouthlike cavern portals and shifts its contours to entrap and beguile adventurers with "inimical volition." Incursions into richly rendered spaces of incessant danger produces an equally apt description for both sword-and-sorcery literature, along with *Dragon's Lair* and its unlikely intertext, D&D.

In its original conception, D&D was a game built around players' incursions into confined and contested places. Successive iterations included expanding rule procedures for exploring vast expanses, often called overworld or hex-crawl adventures, and semi-urban environments, often called town adventure, but the system began as one for underworld adventures, or so-called dungeon crawls. A description of the game's eponymous setting begins the 1983 rule book which plainly states, "a dungeon is a group of rooms where monsters and treasure can be found" (2). This construction, too, became the textual basis for fantasy computer games like *Wizardry*, which was built specifically around a player's descent into a series of deeper and more dangerous dungeons filled with the lure of more resilient antagonists and more valuable loot. A more theoretical portrayal is supplied by the *Advanced Dungeons & Dragons Player Handbook* (Gygax 1978a), which claimed that dungeons are a spatially distributed set of "traps, tricks, and encounters" (103), some pre-established and others randomized by game mechanics. In typical D&D game sessions, players virtually navigate through these spaces, absorb detailed descriptions of their surroundings, and react to environmental dangers. Specifically, the use of traps, violent space-specific dangers, recurs in early gamebooks. *The Tomb of Horrors*, like most of the contemporary game modules, offers a reader a gridded, blueprint-styled map supplemented with numerically coded descriptions for each distinct room, each connected with portals both apparent and secret. This adventure, specifically, is infamous for the unforgiving danger of the traps—pits, false doors, and unseen enemies—that populate the tomb. The game also follows the sword-and-sorcery convention of personifying spatial danger with recurring doorway in the shape of a mouth, which eliminates a player with annihilation if they attempt to pass through. In this, and similar adventures, player survival is highly dependent on quick thinking as well as reflex and luck, the latter of which are part of the game's design via a dice roll called a saving throw. Briefly, saving throws randomize characters' ability to survive, resist, or overcome dangers outside of the player characters' active volition.[11] Again, the comparison of D&D to *Dragon's Lair* seems to demonstrate close correlation as both utilize spatial incursion narratives, segregate space into definable rooms, and punctuate these rooms with both rich detail and environmental dangers where survival is often measured in reflex. I argue that the correlation is informed by their shared antecedent and their respective attempts to adapt it into an early interactive system, one based on paper and the other onscreen. Moreover, the preference for the structure can also be interpreted through the lens of critical theory.

The dungeon crawl, as a combination of the elements of plots of incursion, thick description, and total conflict, is a particular production of space that participates in the fetishization if not celebration of the all-encompassing competition upon which neoliberal reproduction thrives. In the first case, dungeon crawls both accommodate and complicate the individualized ambition of the adventuring protagonist. Remember, Gygax's definition of the dungeon as a place that holds only monsters and treasure. The spatial design of dungeons follows purely the logic of risk and reward and occludes all else that would bespeak a routinization or alternative function of the place. Any more prosaic purpose of built space exists only as bait to lull or deceive interlopers. Nabonidus's banquet hall is merely to lure intruders into vats of poison gas. The temple in the forest was never a place of worship or memorialization but was purpose built to smite jewel thieves. And the blacksmith's shop in *Dragon's Lair* exists only to provide the pretense to hurl a variety of weapons at the player and Dirk. In his own critical assessment of dungeons, Chrulew (2006) claims that the spaces are a textual strategy to reduce the complexity of nature into calculable and eminently controllable systems, presenting users with a playable symptom of domination and colonialism to enjoy. While I am sympathetic to this interpretation, I do not believe that it accounts for the abject peril that sword-and-sorcery players and protagonists confront. What connects the segments of these represented spaces is less any type of rationalization but the logic of a fragmented adventuring, an itinerary of obstacles and a vague goal. Arguably, most videogames of the era normalize this sense of all-pervasive competition as a prescription and description of neoliberal life in its entirety, as discussed above. Here space is imagined as simply the contested receptacle of the obstacles in the way of our individual goals for which we alone are responsible for attaining and for which we alone are guilty in the case that we fail to do so. Sword-and-sorcery provides an important cultural strut which legitimizes this ideological construction, attaches it to desire, and operationalizes it with actions. The dire condition of the dungeon crawl's state of nature also lends logic to the immense individual risk that haunts neoliberal subjects. One wrong move in the "The Tower of the Elephant," in *The Tomb of Horrors*, or the castle of *Dragon's Lair* leads to immediate death, a grim fact undergirding the morbid mood of sword-and-sorcery.

"TO DIE DEALING DEATH"—
SWORD-AND-SORCERY'S GRIM MOOD

There is a long tradition of examining fantastic storytelling as not simply reinforcing or reproducing social order but as offering a redemptive image of social difference. Among his contemporary Marxist critics, Ernst Bloch ([1954] 1995) was unique in his insistence that fantasy and other forms of popular culture were not only commodities to facilitate domination, but just as often were vessels for unfulfilled wishes and desires, or in a word hope. Particularly powerful for Bloch were the stories of cunning little fellows who overcome the shackles of everyday life and use magic objects (symbolizing a non-alienated relationship with things, per Marxist theory) to create entirely new, unexpected futures where order is overturned. Bloch's method is deployed in Jack Zipes (1983) approach to the oral tradition of fairy tales, understood as nascent critiques of power and hierarchy, via images of servants becoming kings and vice versa. The central notion of these claims is also echoed by the work of literary critic Rosemary Jackson (1981) who highlighted fantasy storytelling's ability to tamper with, expose, or break conventions of representational realism and, according to the author, the ideological messaging behind it. But perhaps the most famous analyst of the redemptive function of fantasy was JRR Tolkein who wrote about the form not as a mechanism for social change but for individual recompense in his essay "On Fairy Stories" ([1947] 2001). In the face of what pastoralist Tolkein deemed the unsuitable industrial life of modernity, the author pointed to fantasy's potential to offer recovery from this injurious and trite existence, escape from the prison of everyday sameness, and a joyful consolidation.

This last element constituted what Tolkein called a eucatastrophe, a sudden miraculous grace in the face of seeming impossibility that apologizes for its own absence in everyday life. Eucatastrophe informs the construction of the author's own *Lord of the Rings* which is built to frame the impossible task of Frodo Baggins somehow occurring, and through this occurrence the entire storyworld of Middle-earth is saved or redeemed. Both the overall mood and the conclusions of sword-and-sorcery, preoccupied with the ugliness of violence and inevitability of often pointless death, deny such a redemption. Or, in sword-and-sorcery there is no hope, there is no subversion, and while there may be luck there certainly is no grace.

Echoing this mood, *Dragon's Lair* is a game that went beyond the conventional design and depiction of user deaths and revels in the image of death itself. Videogames, and early arcade games specifically, are uncommon among narrative-informed arts in that the experience most commonly ends in the textual death of the principal character. This is in direct contrast with prior industrialized popular culture formats, like feature films and episodic television series, that relied most on protagonists' twinned professional and romantic success to signal conclusion and cathartic relief. *Dragon's Lair*, as described in chapter 1, treats character death with particular relish. Each of the game's rooms contains the potential of at least one unique sequence animating Dirk's demise as the avatar is flattened by boulders, suffocated by tentacles, impaled by flying swords, etc. All told, including inverted and reused sequences, game footage includes approximately 109 different potential deaths. Moreover, each failed try at the game is bookended by a recurring sequence of a skeletal Dirk flanked by a background field of floating human bones (see fig. 4.6), and each game session concludes with Dirk dropping into frame from screen top, face now greened and shriveled, staring accusingly at the "camera" before dissolving into a collapsing mess of bones (see fig. 4.7). And, as described earlier, a typical player spends a large portion of game time watching these gruesome scenes. I argue that the antecedent of sword-and-sorcery provided a creative template for this grim, morbid mood.

The eventual fates of sword-and-sorcery characters are limited. Earlier I discussed how these characters are constructed as ideal entrepreneurial technocrats, in each story ready for their next gig. But there is another alternative. The possibility of quick, violent death recurs throughout the subgenre. Classical sword-and-sorcery stories contain a dense focus on the graphic vulnerability of the human body, or colloquially they are gory. In part, this tendency is likely overdetermined by the editorial mandate for luridness in pulp production. The macabre fascination also serves a thematic purpose to communicate certain hopelessness, nihilism, or at least pessimism, commonly attributed to Lovecraft but equally present in the work of his colleagues. Howard's work often is punctuated by the bearing of witness of

Figure 4.6   The Field of Skeletons That Punctuates the End of Every Turn in *Dragon's Lair* (2017). *Source*: Screenshot Captured from the Digital Leisure PS4 Port.

Figure 4.7   The Decaying Dirk That Concludes Every Game Session in *Dragon's Lair* (2017). *Source*: Screenshot Captured from the Digital Leisure PS4 Port.

graphic images of non-redemptive death. In "Rogues in the House," Conan calmly watches, via an elaborate periscope device, as several intruders are trapped and, exposed to poison gas, act in a frenzy as, "raging, they fell upon one another with daggers and teeth, slashing, tearing, slaying in a holocaust of madness." Fafhrd and the Grey Mouser, in Leiber's stories, also often act as surrogates witnesses to grim violence. In "Ill Met . . . ," upon their return from the Thieves Guild, they enter Mouser's apartment to find their respective partners killed and devoured by ensorcelled vermin: "although hands and feet had been gnawed bone naked, and bodies tunneled heart deep, the two faces had been spared" (295). But the sword-and-sorcery writer mostly closely associated with the narrative event of character death and the fragility of flesh is Howard and Leiber's contemporary Clark Ashton Smith.

Smith, like Howard, wrote extensively in the sword-and-sorcery tradition for *Weird Tales*, but unlike Howard's work, Smith's stories were not concerned with recurring character but only by shared hyperdiegetic space for the simple, pragmatic reason that Clark's protagonists would rarely survive the events of any single narrative. Death pervades Clark's work in their implied danger and gory imagery as well as an unflattering, de-glamorized inevitability of plot. Smith's "The Seven Geases" contains the author's most complete statement on vainglorious death. In this story, a wizard compels the ostensible protagonist, Ralibar Vooz, to offer himself as a human sacrifice to the ancient god-like entity, Tsathoggua. The creature, however, refuses the gesture and sends Ralibar Vooz similarly to an equally odious, malevolent creature, and the process repeats five more times (therefore, seven geases, or curses). Smith begins the story recounting the heroic deeds and fantastic armaments of the protagonist:

> Ralibar Vooz himself wore a light suiting of copper chainmail, which, flexible as cloth, in no wise impeded his movements. In addition, he carried a buckler made of mammoth-hide with a large bronze spike in its center, that could be used as a thrusting sword; and being a man of huge stature and strength, his shoulders were hung with a whole arsenal of weapons.

This meticulous accounting of martial equipment serves only as ironic juxtaposition as not a single one of these items provides the character with any protection or assistance against his disinterested antagonists. In fact, most of these listed items are doffed with no resistance after the wizard's initial spell. The story promptly concludes after Ralibar Vooz is cursed a seventh time, and in the process of fulfilling the geas, slips and falls into a pit.[12] Six times the protagonist offers sacrifice, an act that can grant meaning and purpose to the act of dying, but no sacrifice is available. The only death available in sword-and-sorcery is a quick, unexpected, inevitable, and ultimately pointless one.

Informed by this morbid mood of sword-and-sorcery, early versions of D&D both in its imagery and its mechanics reiterated this preoccupation of the vulnerability of the body and the inevitability of death. In an examination of the art, book covers and spot illustrations, of early D&D, Greg Gillespie and Darren Crouse (2012) found that the game artists rendered "adventurers as bumbling treasure seekers whose go-for broke attitude meant that starving monsters never went hungry" (448). Further, the authors note, "careless adventurers could expect their tomb-robbing careers [to be] cut radically short in the clutches of a ravenous beast or mechanical trap" (448). Understood now more as a game of prolonged character investment and identification, earlier iterations of D&D contained a player lethality, a thematic death drive, and a likelihood of character death more in accord with the play experience of *Dragon's Lair* as well as the longer tradition of sword-and-sorcery storytelling.

Because all manner of death and bodily dismemberment is ubiquitous to the cultural form of videogames as it has developed, it might be folly to seek too deeply a political-economic motivation for the particularly grim atmosphere of *Dragon's Lair* and other sword-and-sorcery games. However, I argue that the image and conception of death offered by these texts too resonates specifically with the lessons of neoliberal life. The omnipresence of death as a mechanical inevitability and motif of game art reiterates the individualized risks and "get rich or die trying" (here literally) ethos of fantasy adventuring and neoliberal subjecthood alike. The game's many death scenes act to emphatically attach player failure to individual action or inaction, a design technique of side-stepping the overwhelming difficulty of the game. The construction mirrors what Baerg (2009) calls the "ideology of choice," a conservative ideal which suggests that if individuals have a measure of freedom to act, then all responsibility for their eventual fate rests in their own hands alone. Chrulew (2006) in his critique of D&D claimed that that game uses a fictionalized vision of the medieval to construct a play environment where users can act out the condition of what Giorgio Agambem called "bare life," modernity's supplement where existence is ground down to industrial utility, or in the case of the game, down to the question of how much loot or experience does a player get for killing another being. While many videogames approach this asocial formation by designing incentivized combat, *Dragon's Lair* treatment of death is particularly vivid, giving an image of bare life through the utter commonplaceness of death throughout. In this game, death is robbed of its psychic resonance—it's not the transgressive return of the repressed as theorized by many critics of horror imagery; its existential power—it's not a momento mori reminding players of the profound boundaries of existence; and its textual power—character death has no narrative significance beyond the pause of its telling. The repetitive gruesomeness of Dirk's deaths, along with a parade of blood, skulls, and gore of the sword-and-sorcery revival, gives users an image of death alienated from its other cultural meanings and reduced down to its functional utility, a currency to be spent in pursuit of insatiable, manipulated desires, and equivalated with falling quarters. And it is within the pages of classical sword-and-sorcery that we can trace back this unexpected entanglement of the fantastic imagery of the mythical and the mystical with an exceedingly modern nihilism.

NOTES

1. The very fuzziness of terminology and the lack of descriptor for the subgenre serve as further indication of its broad critical dismissal.

2. The promise or more frequently the failed promise of novelty is more a symptom of consumer or popular culture for which it plays the dual functional role of fomenting user demand and facilitating producer ownership.

3. The film concludes on a redemptive note as the Lady of the Lake re-sheaths the eponymous Excalibur in anticipation for its eventual reclaiming played with such excessive pomp, underscored by magic hour lighting, a slow-motion effect of the thrown sword, and the final strains of Wagner's "Siegfried's Funeral March," as to be tempered with authorial irony.

4. Leiber later republished this story under the much less apt title "Jewels in the Forest." Yet even the sparseness of this revised title underscores pecuniary gain as the guiding feature of the principle characters and their exploits.

5. "Ill Met in Lahkmar" earned Leiber the 1971 Nebula award for "best novelette."

6. For example, Peterson discusses, via historical documents like player zines, the question of whether a player with a low intelligence attribute score must act "stupid" during gameplay.

7. "Experience" as a buzzword has a curious resonance with neoliberal critique, as exploited workers in this social order often earn experience for their efforts instead of wages.

8. Arguably, the problematic calculus of justified violence supported by physical excellence can be equally traced to the Western storytelling that pre-dated the sword-and-sorcery tradition in pulp magazine publication.

9. This distaste has been tracked by many looking into the private letters of Howard, but is often openly articulated ad nauseam in his fiction. Nowhere is this feeling more emphatic than in the closing line of "Beyond the Black River" ([1935] 2020) in which Conan, presumably, performs free indirect discourse stating, "[b]arbarism is the natural state of mankind . . . civilization is unnature."

10. Of course, sword-and-sorcery was not the only historical cultural form to encourage this style of being in the world. The logic also informs games based on competitive sports, enshrined in U.S. popular culture and equally present in ported versions in the early videogame arcade.

11. In part, the saving throw could be considered the pen-and-paper equivalent of "twitch" in videogames.

12. Arguably, this fall could be interpreted as a fulfillment of the final geas, which was to seek out the "bleak and drear and dreadful limbo, known as the Outer World"—the implication being that this is precisely what waits for Ralibar Vooz after his death.

References

"A 1983 Chronology of Major Industry Events." *Boxoffice*, May 1, 1984.

A Nation at Risk: The Imperative for Education Reform. A Report to the Nation and the Secretary of Education. Washington DC: Government Printing Office, 1983.

"Abel Launches A.I.R. Expressly for Computer Generated Images." *Backstage*, August 30, 1985.

"Abel Plays Atari for DDB/NY." *Backstage*, October 1, 1982.

"Abel to Host NY Seminars in Efx." *Backstage*, November 2, 1984.

"Abel's Effects Give 7-Up a Lift." *Backstage*, September 10, 1982.

"All Time Film Rental Champs." *Variety*, January 12, 1983.

Allen, Jennifer. "Brave New EPCOT." *New York*, December 20, 1982.

Altman, Ted N. "Video Disc Player with Multiple Signal Recovery Transducers." US Patent 4,386, 375, filed September 24, 1980, and issued May 31, 1983.

Althusser, Louis. *For Marx*, translated by Ben Brewster. London: Verso, 2006.

Amidi, Amid. *Cartoon Modern: Style and Design in 1950s Animation*. New York: Chronicle Books, 2006

Anderson, Christopher. *Hollywood TV: The Studio System in the Fifties*. Austin, TX: University of Texas Press, 1994.

Arenson, Dave, Gary Gygax, and Frank Mentzer. *Dungeons & Dragons Players Manual*. [Lake Geneva, WI]: TSR Hobbies, Inc., 1983.

Arn. "*Dragon's Lair* Arrives for the iPhone." *Touch Arcade*, December 23, 2009. https://toucharcade.com/2009/12/06/dragons-lair-arrives-for-the-iphone/

Arnheim, Rudolph. *Art and Visual Perception: A Psychology of the Creative Eye*. Berkeley: University of California Press, (1941) 2011.

———. *Visual Thinking*. Berkeley: University of California Press. (1969) 2015.

Arnold, G. "Snow White Reawakened." *Washington Post*, July 17, 1983.

Arnold, T. "Space Invaders Being Repelled by Overexposure." *Los Angeles Times*, July 25, 1983.

Arsenault, Dominic. *Super Power, Spoony Bards and Silverware: The Super Nintendo Entertainment System*. Cambridge, MA: MIT Press, 2017.

Attebery, Brian. *The Fantasy Tradition in American Literature*. Bloomingham, IN: Indiana University Press, 1980.

Auerbach, A. "$25,000 Showman Contest." *Boxoffice*, June 1, 1982.

Baer, Ralph. "Dual Image Television." US Patent 3,991,266, filed September 3, 1974, and issued November 9, 1976.

———. "Video Disc Program Branching System." US Patent 4,571,640, filed November 1, 1982, and issued February 18, 1986.

Baer, Ralph and Leonard Cope. "Interactive Playback System." US Patent 4,359,223, filed November 1, 1979, and issued November 16, 1982.

Baerg, Andrew. "Governmentality, Neoliberalism, and the Digital Game." *symploke* 17, no. 102 (2009): 115–127.

Bahktin, M.M. *The Dialogic Imagination: Four Essays*, translated by Caryl Emerson and Michael Holquist. Austin, TX: University of Texas Press, 2014.

Barney, Darin, Gabriella Coleman, Christine Ross, Jonathan Sterne, Tamar Tembeck. "The Participatory Condition: An Introduction." In *The Participatory Condition in the Digital Age*, edited by Barney, Darin, Gabriella Coleman, Christine Ross, Jonathan Sterne, and Tamar Tembeck, vii–xxxix. Minneapolis: University of Minnesota Press, 2016.

Barrier, Michael. *Funnybooks: The Improbable Glories of the Best American Comic Books*. Berkeley, CA: University of California Press, 2015.

Beckerman, H. "Animation Spot." *Back Stage*, July 15, 1983a.

———. "Animation Spot." *Back Stage*, December 2, 1983b.

Beers, George L. "Multiplex Transmission." US Patent 2,874,213, filed June 29, 1954, and issued February 17, 1959.

Best, Robert M. "Dialog Between TV Movies and Human Viewers." US Patent 4,305,131, filed March 31, 1980, and issued December 8 1981.

Bettelheim, Bruno. *The Uses of Enchantment: The Meaning and Importance of Fairy Tales*. New York: Vintage Books, 1975.

Bierbaum, Tom. "Animated 'Lair' Game Renews Interest in Sluggish Field." *Variety*, August 31, 1983.

———. "Laser Game Plan Sees 'Revolution' Heading for Home." *Variety*, February 8, 1984.

Blair, Preston E. and Frank S. Preston. "TV Animation Interactively Controlled by the Viewer." US Patent 4,695,953, filed April 14, 1986, and issued September 22, 1987.

Bloch, Ernst. *The Principle of Hope, Volume 1*, translated by Neville Plaice, Stephen Plaice, and Paul Knight. Cambridge, MA: MIT Press, (1954) 1995.

Bloom, S. "The Lasers Have Landed!" *Computer Games*, April 1984.

"Bluth, Cartoonist Settle Dispute, End Walkout." *Variety*, September 8, 1982.

"Bluth Completes Cartoon Feature." *Variety*, May 19, 1982.

"Bluth Hits Distrib Re *Nimh*; Preps Animated *Canterbury* Pic." *Variety*, December 29, 1982.

"Bluth Relocating Animation Outfit to Ireland; Say Incentives Lure." *Variety*, November 19, 1986.

Boddy, William. *New Media and Popular Imagination: Launching Radio, Television, and Digital Media in the United States*. Oxford: Oxford University Press, 2004.

Bogost, Ian. *Unit Operations: An Approach to Videogame Criticism*. Cambridge, MA: MIT Press, 2006.

———. *How To Talk About Videogames*. Minneapolis, MN: University of Minnesota Press, 2015.

Bogost, Ian and Nick Montfort. *Racing the Beam: The Atari Video Computer System*. Cambridge, MA: MIT Press, 2009.

Boltanski, Luc and Eve Chiapello. *The New Spirit of Capitalism*, translated by Gregory Elliott. London: Verso, 2018.

Bordwell, David. *Making Meaning: Inference and Rhetoric in the Interpretation of Cinema*. Cambridge, MA: Harvard University Press, (1989) 2008.

Bordwell, David, Kristin Thompson, and Janet Staiger. *The Classical Hollywood Cinema: Film Style & Mode of Production to 1960*. New York: Columbia University Press, 1985.

Bown, Alfie. *The Playstation Dreamworld*. London: Wiley, 2017.

Boyer, Steven. "A Virtual Failure: Evaluating the Success of Nintendo's Virtual Boy." *The Velvet Light Trap* 64 (2009): 23–33.

"Branching Out With Classical Style." *Screen International*, July 31, 1982.

Branigan, Edward. *Point of View in the Cinema: A Theory of Narration and Subjectivity in Classical Cinema*. Berlin: De Gruyter, 1984.

Brownstein, M. "The *Computer Games* Interview: Don Bluth." *Computer Games*, April 1984.

Bryant, Anthony. "Liquid Modernity, Complexity and Turbulence." *Theory, Culture, & Society* 24, no. 1 (2007): 127–135.

Burch, Noel. *Theory of Film Practice*, translated by Helen R. Lane. Princeton, NJ: Princeton University Press, 1981

———. "Primitivism and the Avant-Gardes: A Dialectic Approach." In *Narrative, Apparatus, Ideology*, edited by Philip Rosen, 483–506. New York: Columbia University Press, 1986.

Camper, Brett. "Color-cyled Space Fumes in Pixel Particle Shockwave: The Technical Aesthetics of *Defender* and the Williams Arcade Platform, 1980-82." In *Before the Crash: Early Video Game History*, edited by Mark J.P. Wolf, 168–188. Detroit: Wayne State, 2012.

Camras, Marvin. "Magnetic Transducer System." US Patent 3,382,325, filed March 12, 1954, and issued May 7, 1968.

Capcom USA. *Ghosts n' Goblins Instruction Manual*, 1986. http://www.arcade -museum.com/manuals-videogames/G/Ghosts%20N%20Goblins%20Instruction %20Manual.pdf

Cardona, Tarquin. "The New Synergy of Cross-Over Directors." *Backstage*, March 1, 1985.

Carroll, Noel. *Philosophy of Horror: Or, Paradoxes of the Heart*. London: Routledge, (1990) 2015.

"Cartoonist Local First to Authorize Strike Option." *Variety*, July 14, 1982.

Castells, Manuel. *The Rise of the Network Society*. Cambridge, MA: Blackwell, 1996.

Caulfied, D. (1982, Aug. 25). "Disney Vetoes *Nimh* as a Pairing with *Tron*." *Los Angeles Times*, August 25, 1982.

Caves, Richard E. *Switching Channels: Organization and Change in TV Broadcasting*. Cambridge, MA: Harvard University Press, 2005.

Chrulew, Matthew N. "'Masters of the Wild': Animals and the Environment in Dungeons & Dragons." *Concentric* 32, no. 1 (2006): 135–168.

"Coleco Looks Into Laserdisk Add-ons to Home Hardware." *Variety*, September 7, 1983.

Coopersmith, Jonathan. "Failure & Technology." *Japan Journal for Science, Technology & Society* 18 (2009): 93–118.

Costikyan, Greg. "Games, Storytelling, and Breaking the String." *Electronic Book Review*. December 28, 2007. https://electronicbookreview.com/essay/games-story-telling-and-breaking-the-string/

"CPI Shuttering Mylstar Coin-Op Game Division." *Variety*, September 26, 1984.

Crook, D. "Video Game Makers Offering New Twists." *Los Angeles Times*, January 11, 1982.

———. "Animator Leads with a *Space Ace*." *Los Angeles Times*, February 21, 1984a.

———. "Halcyon Days Return with New Hardware." *Los Angeles Times*, December 25, 1984b.

Dardot, Pierre and Christian Laval. *The New Way of the World*, translated by Gregory Elliot. London: Verso, 2014.

Davis, Sally Ogle. "Wishing Upon a Falling Star." *New York Times*, November 16, 1980.

Delany, Samuel. *Tales of Nevèrÿon*. New York: Bantam Books, 1979.

Deleuze, G. *Cinema 1: The Movement Image*, translated by Barbara Habberjam and Hugh Tomlinson. Minneapolis, MN: University of Minnesota, 1986.

———. "Postscript on the Societies of Control." *October* 59, Winter (1992): 3–7.

"Disney Attempts to Reverse Movie Division's Profit Slide." (1981, Aug. 31). *New York Times*, August 31, 1981.

"Disney Exodus and the State of Animation." (1979, Dec. 21). *Back Stage*, December 21, 1979.

Duffy, S. "Coleco in the Cabbage Patch." *Barron's*, December 5, 1983.

Dyer, Richard A. "Full Pictorial Animation Video Game." World Intellectual Property Organization Patent WO 84 / 03792, filed March 15, 1984, and issued September 27, 1984.

Eco, Umberto. *The Open Work*, translated by A. Cancogni and D. Robey. Cambridge, MA: Harvard University Press, 1989.

"Editdroid, Lucasfiilm & Convergence's Joint Venture, Unveiled at NAB." *Backstage*, May 4, 1984.

Edwards, Benj. "The Untold Story of Atari Founder Nolan Bushnell's Visionary 1980s Tech Incubator." *Fast Company*, February 17, 2017. https://www.fastcompany.com/3068135/the-untold-story-of-atari-founder-nolan-bushnells-visionary-1980s-tech-incubator

Ernkvist, Mirko. "Down Many Times, But Still Playing the Game: Creative Destruction and Industry Crashes in the Early Video Game Industry, 1971–1986." *History of Insolvency and Bankruptcy* 38 (2008): 161–191.

Ewalt, David M. *Of Dice and Men: The Story of Dungeons & Dragons and the People Who Play It*. New York: Simon and Schuster, 2013.

Feuer, Jane. "The Conept of Live Television: Ontology as Ideology." In *Regarding Television: Critical Approaches*, edited by E. Ann Kaplan. Los Angeles: AFI, 1983.

Fiske, John. *Television Culture*. London: Routledge, 1987.

Fjellmen, Stephen. *Vinyl Leaves: Walt Disney World and America*. New York: Routledge, 1992.

Forest, Rick. "Is the New Technology Distinguishable from Magic." *Billboard*, January 10, 1981.

"Former Disney Animators Form Independent Co." *Backstage*, September 21, 1979.

Furby, Jaqueline and Claire Hines. *Fantasy*. London: Routledge, 2012.

Galloway, Alexander. *Gaming: Essays on Algorithmic Culture*. Minneapolis, MN: University of Minnesota Press, 2006.

Gantz, J. "Psst...Hot Rumors." *InfoWord*, June 4, 1984.

Gillan, Jennifer. *Television Brandcasting: The Return of the Content-Promotion Hybrid*. London: Routledge, 2015.

Gillespie, Greg and Darren Crouse. "There and Back Again: Nostalgia, Art, and Ideology in Old-School Dungeons and Dragons." *Games and Culture* 7, no. 6 (2012): 441–470.

Girard, T. "Laserdisk Arcade Units Merge Live Pix Plus Graphics." *Variety*, May 11, 1983.

Goldman, Clint. "Abel, Midler, Jagger Team Up." *Backstage*, January 20, 1984a.

———. "Editdroid Nests at Egg Co." *Backstage*, September 7, 1984b.

Goldrich, R. "Animation Newcomer." *Backstage*, November 16, 1979.

———. "Cartoonist Contract." *Back Stage*, September 10, 1982.

Gombrich, E.H. *Art and Illusion: A Study in the Psychology of Pictorial Representation*. London: Phaidon, 1959.

Greenberg, Raz. "The Animation of Gamers and the Gamers as Animators in Sierra On-Line's Adventure Games." *Animation: An Interdisciplinary Journal* 12, no 1–2 (2021): 83–95.

Greenfield, G. "Q-Bert: Development of a Saturday Morning Series." Norman Maurer Papers, 1976–1983 (PASC.0086, Box 31, Folder 25). UCLA Library Special Collections, Performing Arts, Los Angeles, CA, 1983.

Guins, Raiford. *Game After: A Cultural Study of Video Game Afterlife*. Cambridge, MA: MIT Press, 2014.

Guins, Raiford and Henry Lowood. *Debuggging Game History: A Critical Lexicon*. Cambridge, MA: MIT Press, 2016.

Gunning, Tom. "Heard over the Phone: *The Lonely Villa* and the de Lorde Tradition of Terrors of Technology." *Screen* 32, no. 2 (1991): 184–196.

Gutis, P. "Longer Toy Season Sought." *The New York Times*, July 4, 1985.

Gygax, Gary. *Advanced Dungeons & Dragons Players Handbook*. Lake Geneva, WI: TSR Games, 1978a.

———. *Dungeon Module S1: Tomb of Horrors*. Lake Geneva, WI: TSR Games, 1978b.

————. *Advanced Dungeons & Dragons Dungeon Masters Guide*. Lake Geneva, WI: TSR Games, 1979.

Hall, Stuart. "Encoding/Decoding." In *Media Studies: A Reader*, edited by P. Marris & S. Thornham, 51–61. New York: NYU Press, (1973) 2002.

Hanson, Christopher. *Game Time: Understanding Temporality in Video Games*. Bloomington, IN: Indiana University Press, 2018.

Harmetz, A. "Hollywood Playing Harder at the Video Games." *The New York Times*, August 2, 1983.

————. "Video Arcades' New Hope." *The New York Times*, January 20, 1984.

————. "Animation Again a Priority at Disney." *The New York Times*, August 27, 1984.

Harpster, Jack. *King of the Slots: William "SI" Redd*. Santa Barbara, CA: ABC-CLIO, 2010.

Harris, K. "Videodiscs May Give a Powerful Boost to Arcade Games." *Los Angeles Times*, October 2, 1983.

Harvey, David. *A Brief History of Neoliberalism*. Oxford: Oxford University Press, 2005.

Hassenfield, S. "Trying to Run a Bigger Hasbro." *The New York Times*, August 4, 1985.

Hoban, Phoebe. "Responsive TV." *OMNI*, June 1982.

Hollie, P. "The Risky Business of Toys." *The New York Times*, June 27, 1984.

Houghton, William D. "Television Message System for Transmitting Auxiliary Information During the Vertical Blanking Interval of Each Television Field." US Patent 3,493,674, filed May 28, 1965, and issued February 3, 1970.

Howard, Robert E. "Tower of the Elephant." (1933) 2020. https://gutenberg.net.au/ebooks06/0600831h.html

————. "Rogues in the House." (1934) 2020. https://gutenberg.net.au/ebooks06/0600781h.html

————. "Beyond the Black River." (1935) 2020. https://gutenberg.net.au/ebooks06/0600741h.html

————. "Red Nails" (1939) 2020. https://www.gutenberg.org/files/32759/32759-h/32759-h.htm

Hughes, Kit. "Record/Film/Book/Interactive TV: EVR as a Threshold Format." *Television & New Media* 17, no. 1 (2016): 44–61.

Huhtamo, Erkki. "From Kaleidoscomaniac to Cybernerd: Notes Toward an Archeology of the Media." *Leonardo* 30, no. 3 (1997): 221–224.

————. "Slots of Fun, Slots of Trouble. Toward an Archaeology of Electronic Gaming." In *Handbook of Computer Games Studies*, edited by Joost Raessens & Jeffrey Goldstein, 1–21. Cambridge, MA: The MIT Press, 2005.

Huizinga, Johan. *Homo Ludens: A Study of the Play-element in Culture*. Boston, MA: Beacon Press, 1950.

Hurwood, B. "Laserdisc!" *Videogaming & Computing Illustrated*, November 1983.

Involvement in Learning: Realizing the Potential of American Higher Education. A Report to the Nation and the Secretary of Education. Washington DC: Government Printing Office, 1984.

Jackson, Rosemary. *Fantasy: The Literature of Subversion*. London: Routledge, 1981.

Jagoda, Patrick. "Playing Through a Serious Crisis: On the Neoliberal Art of Video Games." *Post45*, August, 31, 2020. https://post45.org/2020/08/playing-through-a -serious-crisis-on-the-neoliberal-art-of-video-games/

Jeffords, Susan. *Hard Bodies: Hollywood Masculinity in the Reagan Era*. New Brunswick, NJ: Rutgers University Press, 1994.

Jenkins, Henry. "Game Design as Narrative Architecture." In *The Game Design Reader: A Rules of Play Anthology*, edited by Katie Salen and Eric Zimmerman, 670–689. Cambridge, MA: MIT Press, 2004.

Jerng, Mark C. *Racial Worldmaking: The Power of Popular Fiction*. New York: Fordham University Press, 2018.

Jones, A. "Rival Gets Milton Bradley." *The New York Times*, May 5, 1985.

Justice, James W.H. "Multiplex Video Transmission System." US Patent 3,725,571, filed on June 21, 1971, and issued April 3, 1973.

Juul, Jesper. "Introduction to Game Time." In *First Person: New Media as Story, Performance, and Game*, edited by Noah Wadrip-Fruin and Pat Harrigan, 131– 142. Cambridge, MA: MIT Press.

Kinder, J. and D. Hallock. *Dragon's Lair Scene Sequencing*. Dragon's Lair Project, n.d. http://www.dragons-lair-project.com/games/related/sequence.asp

Kinney, George C. "Special Purpose Applications of the Optical Videodisc System." *IEEE Transactions on Consumer Electronics* CE-22, no. 4 (1976): 327–338.

Kittler, Friedrich. *Gramophone, Film, Typewriter*, translated by G. Winthrop-Young and M. Wutz. Stanford, CA: Stanford University, (1986) 2006.

———. *Optical Media: Berlin Lectures 1999*, translated by A. Enns. Cambridge, UK: Polity, 2012.

Kleinfield, N. "Video Game Industry Comes Down to Earth." *The New York Times*, October 17, 1983.

———. "Coleco Moves out of the Cabbage Patch." *The New York Times*, July 21, 1985.

Kocurek, Carly A. (2012). "Coin-Drop Capitalism: Economic Lessons from the Video Game Arcade." In *Before the Crash: Early Video Game History*, edited by Mark J.P. Wolf, 189–208. Detroit: Wayne State, 2012.

———. *Coin-Operated Americans: Rebooting Boyhood at the Video Game Arcade*. Minneapolis, MN: University of Minnesota Press, 2015.

Kovacs, Bill. "Creativity Through Computers." *Backstage*, February 29, 1980.

Kreon, Dirk J. and Klaas H.J. Robers. "Device for Interactive Video Playback." US Patent 4,449,198, filed on January 23, 1980, and issued May 15, 1984.

Kuntzel, Thierry. "The Film Work 2." *Camera Obscura* 2, no. 5 (1980): 6–70.

Langshaw, Mark. "*Dragon's Lair* Retrospective: How the Quick Time Even was Born." *Digital Spy*, August 30, 2014. https://www.digitalspy.com/videogames /retro-gaming/a593480/dragons-lair-retrospective-how-the-quick-time-event-was -born/

Lankoski, Petri. *Character-Driven Game Design: A Design Approach and its Foundations in Character Engagement*. Jyväkylä, Finland: Aalto University, Publication Series of the School of Art and Design, 2010.

Latour, Bruno. "Technology is Society Made Durable." *The Sociological Review* 38, no. 1 (1990): 103–131.

———. *Re-assembling the Social: An Introduction to Actor-network Theory*. Oxford: Oxford University Press, 2005.

Latour, Bruno and Steve Woolgar. *Laboratory Life: The Construction of Scientific Facts*. Princeton, NJ: Princeton University Press, 2013.

Leiber, Fritz. "Jewels in the Forest." In *Swords Against Death*, 20–62. New York: Ace Publishing Corporation, (1939) 1970.

———. "Ill Met in Lankhmar." In *Swords and Deviltry*, 163–254. New York: Ace Fantasy Books, (1970) 1983.

Lessard, Jonathan. "*Fahrenheit* and the Premature Burial of Interactive Movies." *Eludamos. Journal for Computer Game Culture* 3, no. 2 (2009): 195–205.

Levi-Strauss, Claude. "Structural Study of Myth." *Journal of American Folklore* 68, no. 270 (1955): 428–444.

Levinsohn, Craig I. "Creativity Reigns at Abel & Assocs. for All Media." *Backstage*, September 10, 1982.

Lipartito, Kenneth. Picturephone and the Information Age: The Social Meaning of Failure. *Technology and Culture* 44, no. 1 (2003): 50–81.

"Local 839 Okays Pact, But Disney's Animators Hold Off." *Variety*, September 22, 1982.

Lohwood, Henry. "Video Games in Computer Space: The Complex History of *Pong*." *IEEE Annals of the History of Computing* 31, no. 3 (2009): 5–19.

"Lucasfilm Unveils Logic Design System." *Computerworld*. December 19, 1983.

McCullaugh, Jim. "Videomusic: Creating a New Art for a New Industry." *Billboard*, November 22, 1980.

Manovich, Lev. *The Language of New Media*. Cambridge, MA: MIT Press, 2001.

Mataes, Michael and Andrew Stern. "Interaction and Narrative." In *The Game Design Reader: A Rules of Play Anthology*, edited by Katie Salen and Eric Zimmerman, 642–669. Cambridge, MA: MIT Press, 2004.

Mathieu, Michel. "A Random Access System Adapted for the Optical Videodisc: Its Impact on Information Retrieval." *SMPTE Journal* 86 (1977): 80–83.

Matthews, Richard. *Fantasy: The Liberation of Imagination*. London: Routledge, 2011.

Mayne, Judith. *Cinema and Spectatorship*. London: Routledge, 1993.

Mertens, Jacob. Broken Games and the Perpetual Update: Revising Failure with Ubisoft's *Assassin's Creed Unity*. *Games and Culture* (2021). doi:10.1177/15554120211017044.

Mes, Johannes Antonius Maria. "Information Carrier Having Addressed Information Tracks." US Patent 3,931,457, filed March 26, 1973, and issued January 6, 1976.

Metz, Christian. *The Imaginary Signifier*, translated by Celia Britton, Annwyl Williams, Ben Brewster, and Alfred Guzzetti. Bloomington, IN: Indiana University Press, 1982.

Mills, B. "Disney Looks for a Happy Ending to its Grim Fairy Tale." *American Film*, July 1, 1982.

[MGM/UA Ad]. *Boxoffice*, June 1, 1982.

Moorcock, Michael. *Elric of Melniboné*, 3–54. New York: Ace Books (1972) 1987.

———. *Wizardry & Wild Romance: A Study of Epic Fantasy*. Austin, TX: Monkeybrain, Inc., 2004.

Moriarty, Colin. "*Dragon's Lair* Review." *IGN*, May 4, 2012. https://www.ign.com/articles/2010/11/29/dragons-lair-review

Morningstar, Gersh. "EPCOT Disney and Ma Bell: Our Future? Maybe That's Not So Good." *Emmy*, May/June 1983.

Murphy, A. "'82 Film B.O. Up 16% to $3.449." *Variety*, January 12, 1983.

"NAB '84: The Year of the Computer." *Broadcasting*, May 14, 1984.

Naisbitt, John. *Megatrends: Ten New Directions Transforming Our Lives*. New York: Warner Books, 1982.

"New Black Box by Bushnell for Interactive TV." *Backstage*. December 23, 1983.

Newman, James A. "The Myth of the Ergodic Videogame: Some Thoughts on Player-Character Relationships in Videogames." *Game Studies* 2, no. 1 (2002). http://www.gamestudies.org/0102/newman/

———. *Videogames*. London: Routledge, 2004.

Newman, Michael Z. *Atari Age: The Emergence of Video Games in America*. Cambridge, MA: MIT Press, 2017.

O'Grady, David. "Movies in the Gameworld: Revisiting the Video Game Cutscene and Its Temporal Implications." In *The Game Culture Reader*, edited by Jason C. Thompson and Marc A. Ouelllette, 103–124. Newcastle upon Tyne: Cambridge Scholars Publishing, 2013.

Overpeck, Deron. "The New Hollywood, 1981-1999: Editing." In *Editing and Special / Visual Effects*, edited by Charlie Keil and Kristen Whissel, 129–141. New Brunswick, NJ: Rutgers University Press, 2016.

Parikka, Jussi. *What is Media Archeology?* Malden, MA: Polity Press, 2012.

Perlmutter, David. *American Toons In: A History of Television Animation*. Jefferson, NC: McFarland, 2014.

Perron, Bernard. Silent Hill: *The Terror Engine*. Ann Arbor, MI: University of Michigan Press, 2012.

Perron, Bernard, Dominic Arsenault, Martin Picard, and Carl Therrien. "Methodological Questions in 'Interactive Film Studies'." *New Review of Film and Television Studies* 6, no. 3 (2008): 233–252.

Peterson, Jon. *The Elusive Shift: How Roleplaying Games Forged Their Identity*. Cambridge, MA: MIT Press, 2020.

Pinchbeck, Daniel. Doom: *Scarydarkfast*. Ann Arbor, MI: University of Michigan Press, 2013.

"Play Now, Play Laser." *Electronic Fun*, February, 1984.

Prince, Stephen. *A New Pot of Gold: Hollywood Under the Electronic Rainbow*. Berkeley, CA: University of California Press, 2000.

Propp, Vladimir. *The Russian Folktale*, translated by S. Forrester. Detroit: Wayne State University Press, (1958) 2012.

Pursell, Carroll. "Technologies as Cultural Practice and Production." *Technology and Culture* 51, no. 3 (2010): 715–722.

Robley, L. and B. Kunkel. "Games on Disc." *Electronic Games*, January 1984.

Rodesch, Dale. "Interactive System and Method for the Control of Video Playback Devices." US Patent 4,422,105, filed September 30, 1980, and issued December 20, 1983.

———. "Interactive Video Disc System." US Patent 4,475,132, filed January 22, 1982, and issued October 4, 1984.

Ruggill, Judd Ethan and Ken S. Mcallister. Tempest: *Geometries of Play*. Ann Arbor, MI: University of Michigan Press, 2015.

Ryan, Marie-Laure. "Immersion vs. Interactivity: Virtual Reality and Literary Theory." *Postmodern Culture* 5, no. 1 (1994): 110–137.

"Sale of Knickerbocker Assets to Give WCI 40% of Hasbro Toys." *Variety*, December 1, 1982.

Salmans, S. "Christmas is a Video Game." *The New York Times*, December 6, 1981.

San Bernardino Sun. "Solid State's Efficiency Improves Gambling Devices." August 15, 1976.

Sandler, Kevin. "Limited Animation, 1947–1989." In *Animation*, edited by Scott Curtis, 75–102. New Brunswick, NJ: Rutgers University Press, 2019.

Sanger, E. "Playing for Keeps: Milton Bradley Enters the Video Game." *Barron's*, April 25, 1983.

Saunders, Charles R. "'Die, Black Dog!': A Look at Racism in Fantasy Literature." (1975) 2001. http://www.reindeermotel.com/CHARLES/charles_blog42_die-blackdog.html

Saunders, Charles R. *Imaro*. San Francisco: Nightshade Press, (1981) 2006.

Shaviro, Steven. *Post Cinematic Affect*. Winchester, UK: 0 [Zero] Books. 2010.

Skelly, Tim. "Rise and fall of Cinematronics." In *Before the Crash: Early Video Game History*, edited by Mark J.P. Wolf, 138–167. Detroit: Wayne State, 2012.

Slater, Michael. "Zilog Oral History Panel on the Founding of the Company and the Development of the Z80 Microprocessor." *Computer History Museum*. April 27, 2007. http://archive.computerhistory.org/resources/access/text/2015/06/102658073-05-01-acc.pdf

Slusser, Gary. "Introduction." In *Unearthly Visions: Approaches to Science Fiction and Fantasy Art*, edited by Gray Westfahl, George Slusser, and Kathleen Church Plummer. Westport, CT: Greenwood Press, 2002.

Smith, Clark Ashton. "The Ice-Demon." (1933) 2006. http://www.eldritchdark.com/writings/short-stories/96/the-ice-demon

———. "The Seven Geases." (1934) 2007. http://www.eldritchdark.com/writings/short-stories/192/the-seven-geases

Smith, Greg M. "A Few Words About Interactivity." In *On a Silver Platter: CD-ROMs and the Promises of a New Technology*, edited by Greg M. Smith. New York: NYU Press, 1999.

Smith, Mark. "[*Dragon's Lair HD* Review]." *Game Lite Chronicles*. October 3, 2006. http://www.gamechronicles.com/reviews/pc/dlairhd/dlairhd.htm

Smuts, Aaron. "What is Interactivity?" *The Journal of Aesthetic Education* 43, no. 4 (2009): 53–73.

Solomon, Charles. "Will the Real Walt Disney Please Stand Up?" *Film Comment* 18, no. 4 (1982): 49–54.

———. "Lucasfilm Introduces a High-tech Editing Tool." *Los Angeles Times*, August 25, 1984.

Sobchack, Vivian. *Screening Space: The American Science Fiction Film*. New Brunswick, NJ: Rutgers University Press, 1997.

Spigel, Lynn. *Make Room for TV: Television and the Family Ideal in Postwar America*. Chicago, IL: University of Chicago Press, 1992.

Stang, Sarah, and Aaron Trammel. "The Ludic Bestiary: Misogynistic Tropes of Female Monstrosity in *Dungeons & Dragons*." *Games and Culture* 15, no. 6 (2020): 730–747.

Stevenson, R. "The Selling of Toy 'Concepts'." *The New York Times*, December 14, 1985.

Stilpen, Scott. "DP Interviews: Paul Allen Newell." *Digital* Press, 2008. http://www .digitpress.com/library/interviews/interview_paul_allen_newell.html

Stine, Kyle and Axel Volmar. "Infrastructures of Time: An Introduction to Hardwired Temporalities." In *Media Infrastructures and the Politics of Digital Time: Essays on Hardwired Temporalities*, edited by Kyle Stine and Axel Volmar, 9–37. Amsterdam: University of Amsterdam Press, 2021.

Streeter, Thomas. *The Net Effect: Romanticism, Capitalism, and the Internet*. New York: NYU Press, 2010.

Summers, J. "Disney Alum Prescribes Cure for Animation's Ills?" *Boxoffice*, March 17, 1980.

Sweeting, James. "*Dragon's Lair Trilogy* Review." *Switch Player*, March 4, 2019. https://switchplayer.net/2019/03/04/dragons-lair-trilogy-review/

"Taking the Zing out of the Arcade Business." *New York Times*, October 24, 1982.

Toffler, Alvin. *Third Wave*. New York: Bantam Books, 1980.

Tolkein, J.R.R. "On Fairy-Stories." In *Tree and Leaf*, 1–82. New York: Harper Collins, (1947) 2001.

Trammel, Aaron. *Roleplaying Game Studies: A Transmedia Approach*. London: Routledge, 2018.

Turnock, Julie A. *Plastic Reality: Special Effects, Technology, and the Emergence of 1970s Blockbuster Aesthetics*. New York: Columbia University Press, 2015.

Tusher, W. "Prominent Risk Warning Given to Aurora's $5,000 Pic Units." *Variety*, April 29, 1981.

"12 Animators Leave Disney to Form Independent Co." *Boxoffice*, October 1, 1979.

United States International Trade Commission. "A Competitive Assessment of the U.S. Video Game Industry: USITC Publication 1501." Washington, DC: Government Printing Office, March 1984.

Vartan, V. "The Strength of Toy Stocks." *The New York Times*, November 8, 1985.

Voorhees, Gerald. "Neo-liberal Multiculturalism in *Mass Effect*: The Government of Difference in Digital RPGs." In *Dungeons, Dragons, and Digital Denizens: The Digital Role-Playing Game*, edited by Gerald Voorhees, Josh Call, and Katie Whitlock, 259–277. New York: Continuum, 2012.

Warga, Wayne. "Disney Films: Chasing the Changing Times." *Los Angeles Times*, October 26, 1980.

"Warners Communications Sets 14 Bank Agreement." *Variety*, April 10, 1985.

"Warner Unloads Atari." *Broadcasting*, July 9, 1983.

Wasko, Janet. *Hollywood in the Information Age: Beyond the Silver Screen*. Austin, TX: University of Texas Press, 1994.

———. *Understanding Disney*. Malden, MA: Polity Press, 2001.

Wasser, Frederick. *Vini, Vidi, Video: The Hollywood Empire and the VCR*. Austin, TX: University of Texas Press, 2001.

"What's New in Products, Services, and Literature." *American Cinematographer*, October 1981.

Winslow, Ken. "Fast Forward." *Billboard*, April 14, 1984.

———. "Advances in Computer Editing." *Billboard*, July 14, 1984.

Witwer, Michael. *Empire of Imagination: Gary Gygax and the Birth of Dungeons and Dragons*. New York: Bloomsbury, 2015.

Wolf, Mark J.P. "Inventing Space: Toward and Taxonomy of On- and Off-screen Space in Video Games." *Film Quarterly* 51, no. 1 (1997): 11–23.

———. "Assessing Interactivity in Video Game Design." *Mechademia: Second Arc* 1 (2006): 78–85.

———. *Building Imaginary Worlds: The Theory and History of Subcreation*. London: Routledge, 2012a.

———. "Introduction." In *Before the Crash: Early Video Game History*, edited by Mark J.P. Wolf, 1–8. Detroit: Wayne State, 2012.

Wollen, Peter. "Godard and Counter Cinema: *Vent D'est*." In *Narrative, Apparatus, Ideology*, edited by Philip Rosen, 120–129. New York: Columbia University Press, 1986.

Wood, Robin. *Hollywood from Vietnam to Reagan . . . and Beyond*. New York: Columbia University Press, 2003.

Wyatt, Justin. *High Concept: Movies and Marketing in Hollywood*. Austin, TX: University of Texas Press, 1994.

Zielski, Siegfried. *Deep Time of the Media: Toward and Archeology of Hearing and Seeing by Technical Means*, translated by Timothy Druckrey. Cambridge, MA: MIT Press, 2006.

Zipes, Jack. *Fairy Tales and the Art of Subversion*. London: Heinemann, 1983.

———. *The Irresistible Fairy Tale: The Cultural and Social History of a Genre*. Princeton, NJ: Princeton University Press, 2013.

Zuckerman, Faye. "Turtles Pacing New Videodisk Adventure Game." *Billboard*, March 3, 1984.

Index

About the Author

MJ Clarke is an associate professor in TV, Film, and Media Studies at California State University, Los Angeles. He teaches and writes about television, comic books, video games, and popular culture. His book *Transmedia Television* investigated the organizational and artistic changes occurring in early twentieth-century U.S. network television, and his previous essays have appeared in *Television and New Media*, *Games and Culture*, and *The Journal of Graphic Novels and Comics*.

Lightning Source UK Ltd.
Milton Keynes UK
UKHW051312080622
404123UK00003B/21